Name_____

Follow directions to finish this picture.

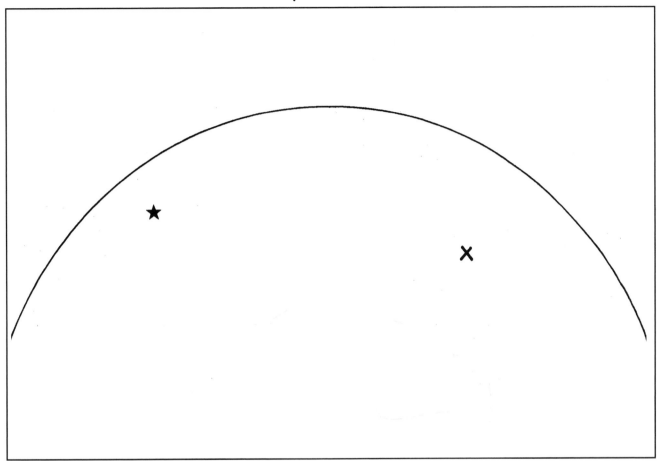

Color. Cut out. Paste.

Paste on the ★.

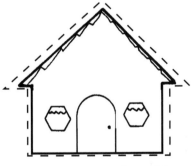

Paste on the **X**.

Paste above the .

Paste on the .

Paste over the .

Paste on the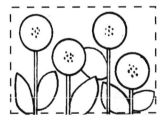

Beginning Reading Activities • EMC 5305

Colorea las cosas de comer de color **amarillo**.

Colorea las prendas de vestir de color **rojo**.

Colorea las cosas en que se puede viajar de color **azul**.

Colorea las cosas en que podemos sentarnos de color **verde**.

Name_____

Color things to eat **yellow**.

Color things to wear **red**.

Color things to ride **blue**.

Color things to sit on **green**.

 Beginning Reading Activities • EMC 5305

Nombre _____

Completa el dibujo.

Pon estas casas en la pecera:

agua   3 pececitos rojos
3 plantas verdes   2 peces dorados grandes
arena   un caracol

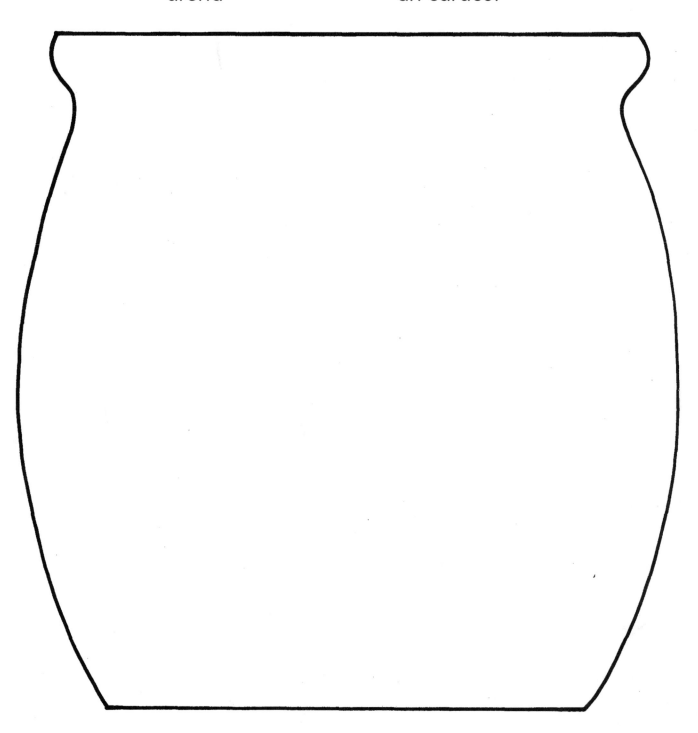

Name_____

Complete the picture.

Put these in your fishbowl:

water   3 small red fish
3 green plants   2 large goldfish
sand   a snail

Nombre _____

Sigue estas instrucciones:

1. Busca el abrigo. Píntalo rojo. Enciérralo en un cuadrado.
2. Busca el pajaro. Píntalo verde. Márcalo con una X.
3. Busca el barco. Píntalo azul y amarillo.
4. Busca el calcetín. Píntalo morado. Enciérralo en un cuadrado.
5. Busca la ballena. Píntala de negro. Márcala con una X.
6. Busca la carreta. Píntala roja y negra.
7. Busca el sombrero. Píntalo anaranjado. Enciérralo en un cuadrado.
8. Busca la vaca. Píntala color café. Márcala con una X.
9. Busca el carrito. Píntalo azul y negro.
10. Pon estrellas anaranjadas en la fruta.

Name_____

Follow these directions.

1. Find the coat. Make it red. Make a box around it.
2. Find the bird. Make it green. Make an **X** on it.
3. Find the boat. Make it blue and yellow.
4. Find the sock. Make it purple. Make a box around it.
5. Find the whale. Make it black. Make an **X** on it.
6. Find the wagon. Make it red and black.
7. Find the hat. Make it orange. Make a box around it.
8. Find the cow. Make it brown. Make an **X** on it.
9. Find the car. Make it blue and black.
10. Make orange stars on the fruit.

Nombre_____

Completa el monstruo.

3 ojos de color morado	una boca con dientes afilados
una nariz extraña	cabello de color anaranjado
orejas grandes y puntiagudas	manchas

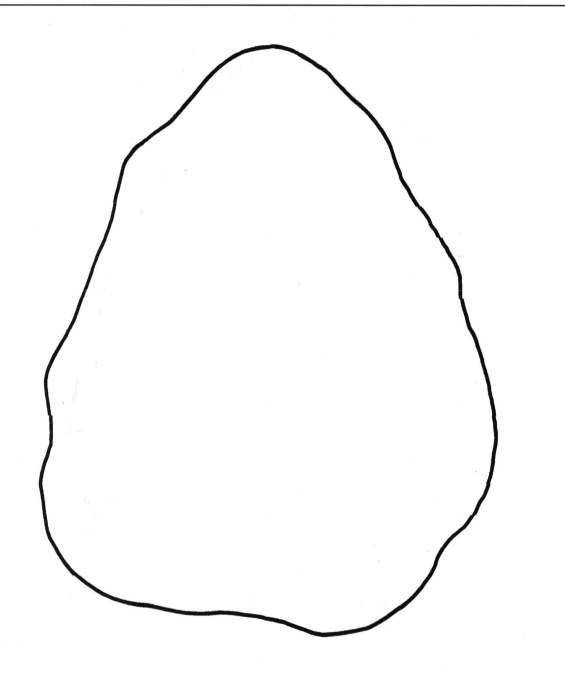

El nombre de mi monstruo es _____ .

Vive _____ .

Name_____

Complete this monster.

3 purple eyes	a mouth with sharp teeth
a strange nose	orange hair
big, pointed ears	spots

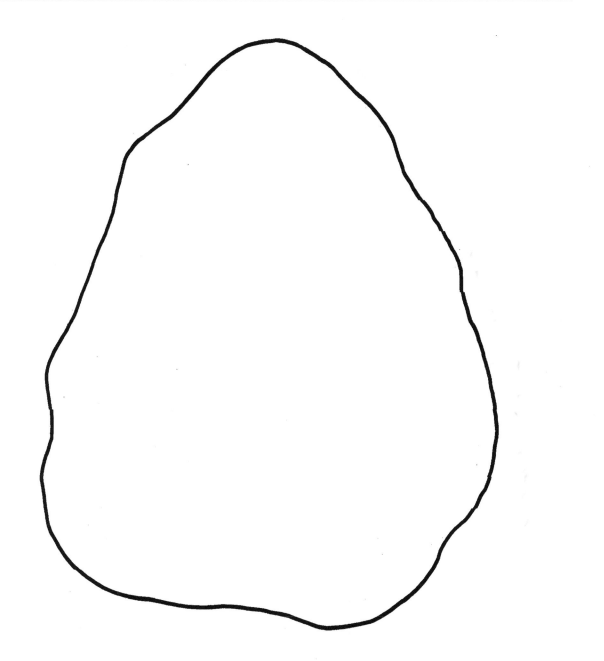

My monster's name is _____ .

It lives_____ .

Nombre _____

Recorta y pega.

12

Name_____

Cut and paste:

13

Nombre_____

Convierte este círculo en...

un juguete

alguna comida

algo donde puedes viajar

una prenda de vestir

una persona

un animal

Ahora:
Toma una hoja de papel.
Escribe una oración sobre cada dibujo.

Name_____

Turn this shape into...

a toy	some kind of food
something to ride	something to wear
a person	an animal

Now:
Get a sheet of paper.
Write a sentence about each picture.

         Beginning Reading Activities • EMC 5305

Nombre _____

Usa la clave para contestar la adivinanza.

¿Por qué el elefante se pinta de rojo las uñas?

a - 1	e - 6	j - 11	n - 16	r - 21	v - 26
b - 2	f - 7	k - 12	ñ - 17	rr - 22	w - 27
c - 3	g - 8	l - 13	o - 18	s - 23	x - 28
ch - 4	h - 9	ll - 14	p - 19	t - 24	y - 29
d - 5	i - 10	m - 15	q - 20	u - 25	z - 30

19	1	21	1

19	18	5	6	21

6	23	3	18	16	5	6	21	23	6

6	16

25	16

3	1	15	19	18

5	6

7	21	6	23	1	23

Name_____

Use the code to answer the riddle.

Why does an elephant paint her toenails red?

a - 1	e - 5	i - 9	m - 13	q - 17	u - 21	y - 25
b - 2	f - 6	j - 10	n - 14	r - 18	v - 22	z - 26
c - 3	g - 7	k - 11	o - 15	s - 19	w - 23	
d - 4	h - 8	l - 12	p - 16	t - 20	x - 24	

19	15

19	8	5

3	1	14

8	9	4	5

9	14

1

19	20	18	1	23	2	5	18	18	25

16	1	20	3	8

Nombre_____

Haz una lista de 20 animales.

1. _____   11. _____

2. _____   12. _____

3. _____   13. _____

4. _____   14. _____

5. _____   15. _____

6. _____   16. _____

7. _____   17. _____

8. _____   18. _____

9. _____   19. _____

10. _____   20. _____

Ahora...
   Encierra con círculo los nombres de mascotas: (gato)
   Encierra con cuadrado los nombres de animales de granja: [vaca]
   Pon una **X** en los nombres de animales salvajes: ~~jirafa~~

Dibuja un animal en cada cuadrado.

mascota	animal de granja	animal salvaje

Name_____

List 20 animals.

1. _____ 11. _____

2. _____ 12. _____

3. _____ 13. _____

4. _____ 14. _____

5. _____ 15. _____

6. _____ 16. _____

7. _____ 17. _____

8. _____ 18. _____

9. _____ 19. _____

10. _____ 20. _____

Now...
Circle the pet words: (cat)
Box the farm animal words: [cow]
X the wild animal words: giraffe

Draw one animal in each box.

pet	farm animal	wild animal

Nombre _____

Sigue las instrucciones.

Había una viejecita que se tragó _____

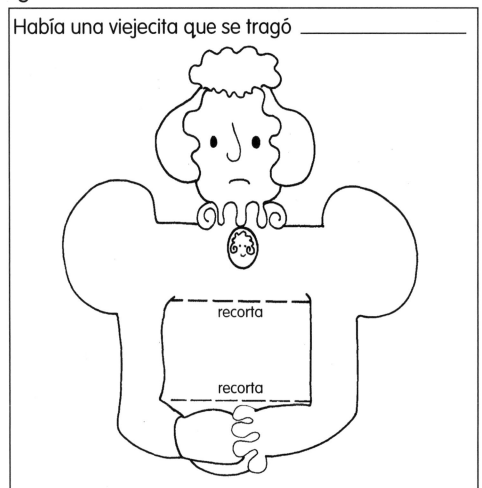

recorta

recorta

jala

Colorea la viejecita:
cabello canoso   ojos azules   vestido rojo

Colorea los animales:
1. mosca - negra   5. caballo - negro
2. vaca - morada   6. gato - amarillo
3. perro - café   7. pájaro - rojo
4. araña - anaranjada   8. chivo - café

Recorta - - - - - - - - - - - - - -

¡Pasa la tira de animales por el estómago de la viejecita y canta!

jala

Name_____

Follow the directions.

There was an old lady who swallowed a _____ .

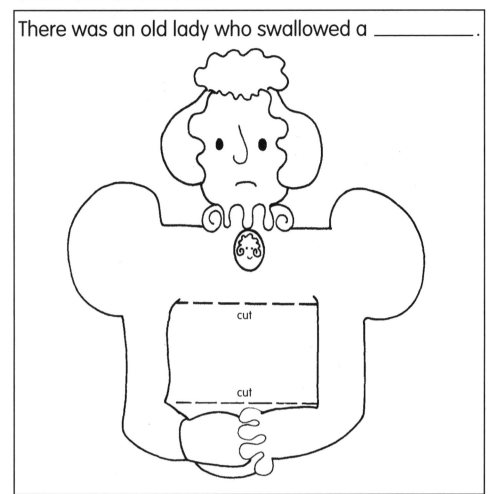

A. Color the old woman:
   gray hair   blue eyes   red dress

B. Color the animals:
1. fly - black   5. horse - black
2. cow - purple   6. cat - yellow
3. dog - brown   7. bird - red
4. spider - orange   8. goat - tan

C. Cut - - - - - - - -

D. Weave the strip of animals through the old
   lady's tummy and sing along!

                   Beginning Reading Activities • EMC 5305

Nombre _____

Completa el dibujo:

La cara alegre: pelo rojo, sombrero negro, corbata amarilla con puntos azules

La cara triste: cinta azul, pelo amarillo, ojos verdes, collar dorado

La cara asustada: corbata verde, pelo negro, gorra anaranjada y verde

La cara enojada: pelo café rizado, mejillas rojas, barba café

La cara dormilona: gorrito de bebé, boquita rosada, pecas color café

Name_____

Complete the picture:

Happy face: red hair, black hat, yellow tie with blue dots

Sad face: blue ribbon, yellow hair, green eyes, gold necklace

Scared face: green tie, black hair, orange and green cap

Angry face: brown curly hair, red cheeks, brown beard

Sleepy face: baby bonnet, pink mouth, brown freckles

Beginning Reading Activities • EMC 5305

Nombre_____

Completa el dibujo.

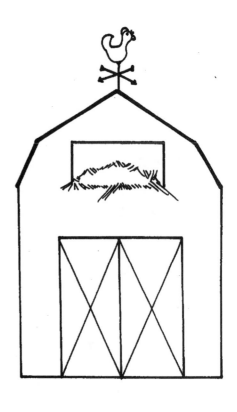

_____ Dibuja una cerca al lado del establo.

_____ Pon una vaca detrás de la cerca.

_____ Haz un grupo de gallinas en frente de la cerca.

_____ Dibuja un granjero dando de comer a las gallinas.

_____ Pinta la camisa del granjero amarilla y su sombrero
           color café.

_____ Pon un perrito dormido al lado de la puerta del establo.

_____ Colorea el dibujo.

Name_____

List your 10 favorite foods:

1._____   6._____

2._____   7._____

3._____   8._____

4._____   9._____

5._____   10._____

Now mark each category like this:

meat

fruit   all other foods

Draw your favorite food here.

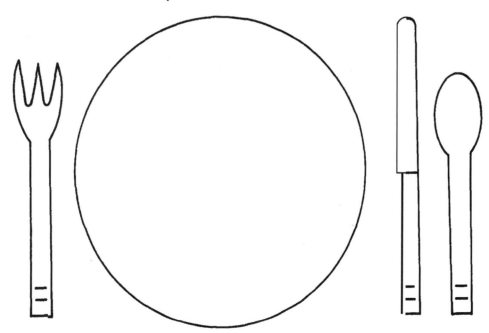

Usa estas formas geométricas para hacer un ser extraño.

Pega tu creación en otro papel.

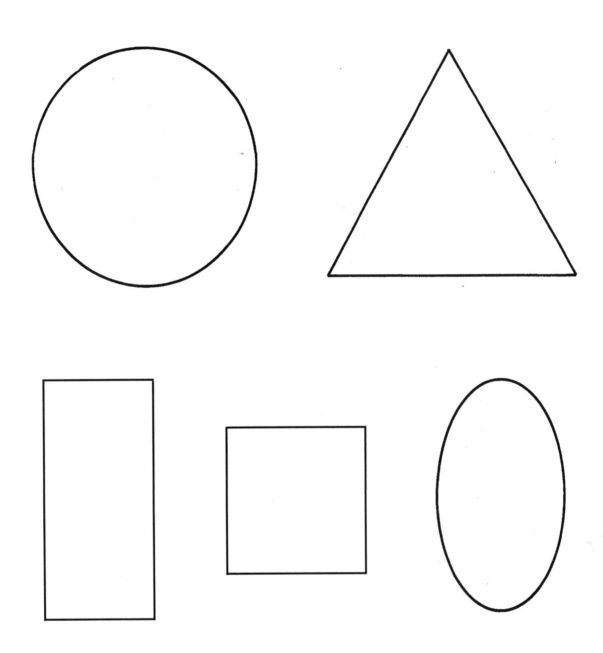

Toma un papel de escribir.
Dale un nombre a lo que inventaste.
Menciona tres cosas que puede hacer.

Name_____

Use these shapes to create an unusual creature.

Paste it to another piece of paper.

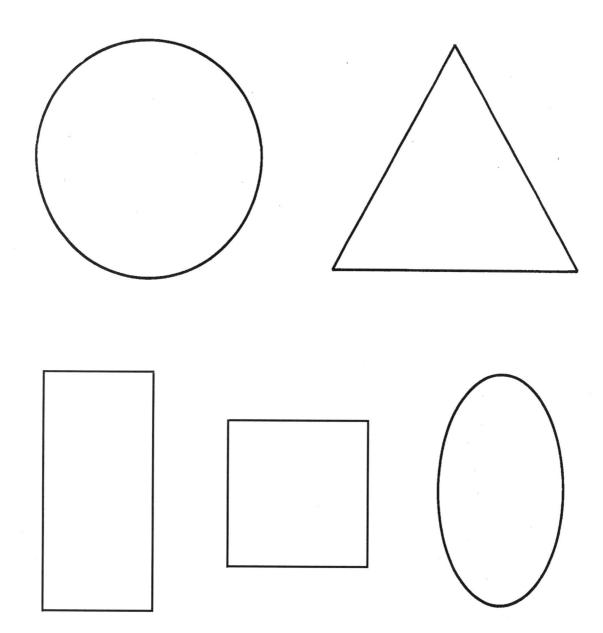

Get a sheet of writing paper.
Name your creature.
Tell three things it can do.

Nombre _____

Colorea:

nombres de números - morado
nombres de los colores - rojo
nombres de niños - negro
nombres de niñas - amarillo

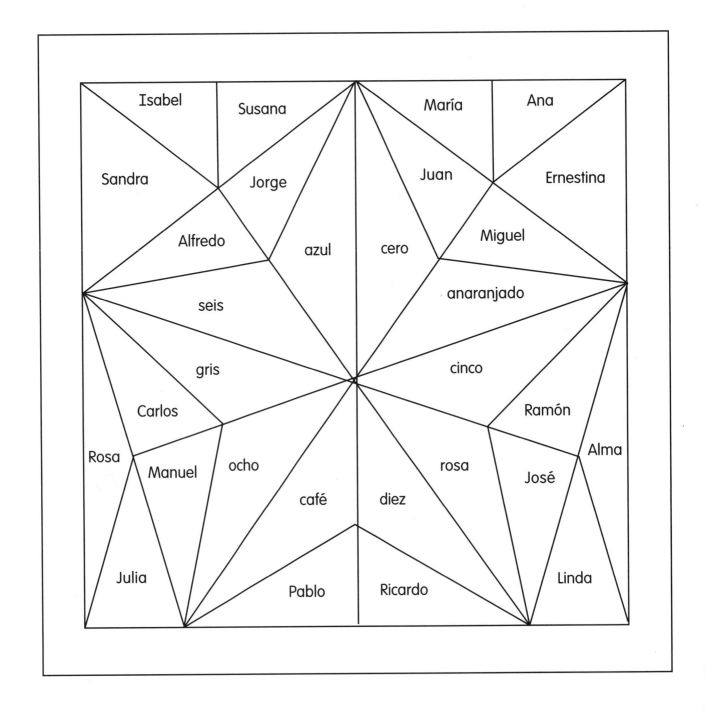

Name_____

Color:

number names - purple
color words - red
boys' names - black
girls' names - yellow

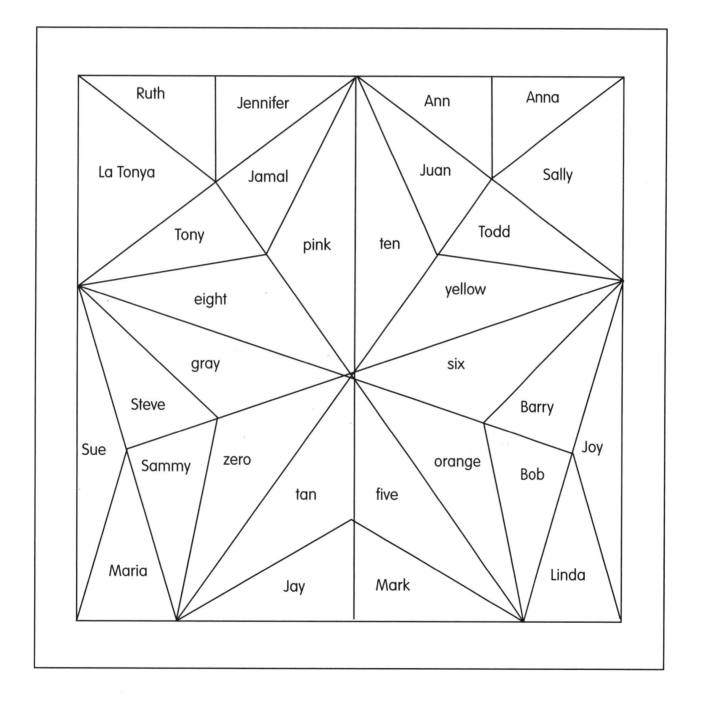

Nombre _____

Sigue las instrucciones para hacer un pez.

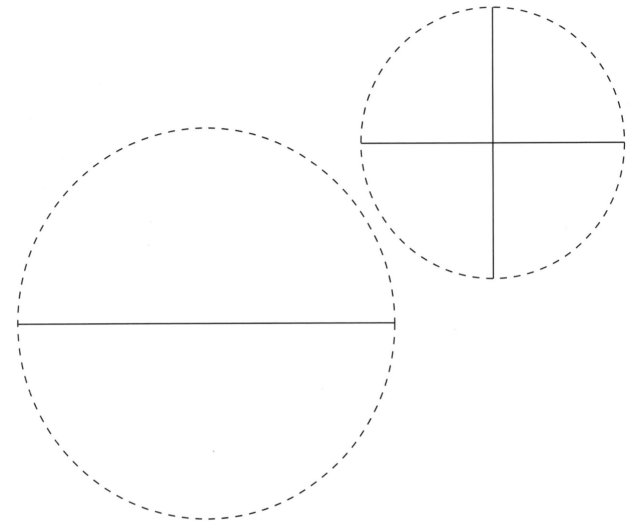

1. Colorea los círculos con tu color favorito.

2. Corta sobre éstas lineas: – – – – –. Dobla sobre éstas líneas: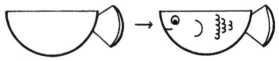

3. Pega la cola en el cuerpo.

4. Añade un ojo, la boca, las agallas y las escamas.

5. Pega tu pez en papel azul y dibuja:

burbujas   plantas verdes   arena y piedras

Name_____

Follow the directions to make a fish.

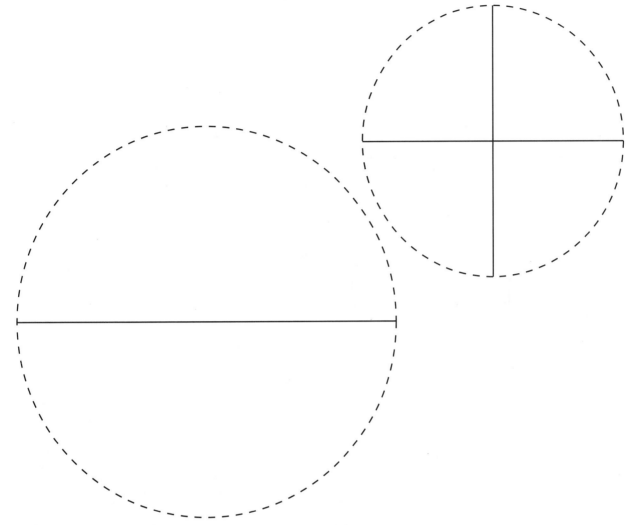

1. Color the circles your favorite color.

2. Cut on the - - - - - -lines. Fold on the ———lines.

3. Paste the tail to the body.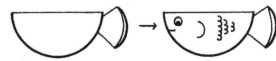

4. Add an eye, mouth, gills, and scales.

5. Paste your fish to blue paper and draw:

bubbles

green plants

sand and rocks

33 Beginning Reading Activities • EMC 5305

Nombre _____

Colorea los cuadrados para contenstar la adivinanza.

△ azul   • negro

Tengo miedo de mi sombra.
¿Quién soy?

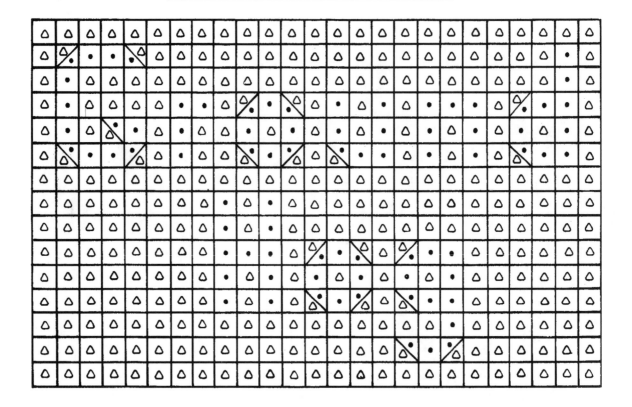

¿Puedes dibujarme escondiéndome en mi madriguera?

Name_____

Color the boxes to answer the riddle.

△ blue   • black

| I am afraid of my shadow. |
| Who am I? |

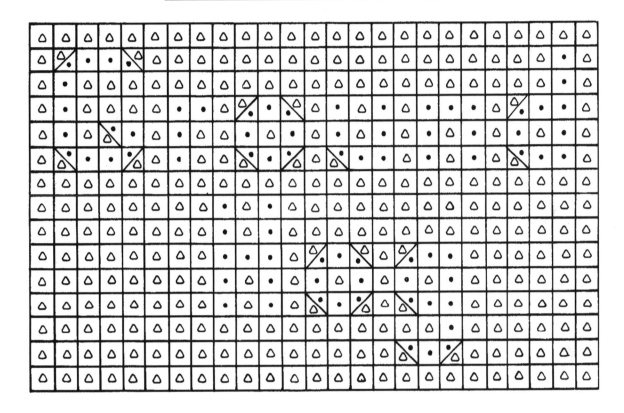

Can you draw me hiding in my burrow?

Nombre_____

Sigue las instrucciones.
Colorea cada cuadrado para hacer un dibujo.

16	11	3	12
azul con un pez morado	rojo	blanco / amarillo	rojo / blanco

9	7	15	10
rojo / blanco	amarillo con un sol anaranjado	azul	rojo

13	8	2	14
azul	blanco / amarillo	blanco / verde	azul

1	2	3	4
5	6	7	8
9	10	11	12
13	14	15	16

Name_____

Follow the directions.
Color each box to make a picture.

16	11	3	12
blue with a purple fish	red	white / yellow	red / white

9	7	15	10
red / white	yellow with an orange sun	blue	red

13	8	2	14
blue	white / yellow	white / green	blue

1	2	3	4

5	6	7	8

9	10	11	12

13	14	15	16

Beginning Reading Activities • EMC 5305

Nombre _____

Sigue las instrucciones para hacer una máscara.

1. Usa un papel de colores que mide 9" x 12".

2. Recorta: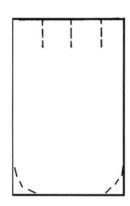

Guarda las esquinas para las orejas.

3. Riza el pelo. Pega las orejas.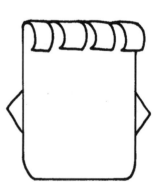

4. Recorta los ojos y una nariz.
   Colorea la cara.
   Dibuja la boca.

Ejemplos: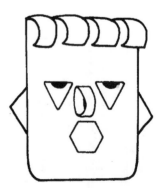

Name_____

Follow the directions to make a mask.

1. Get out a 9″ X 12″ sheet of colored paper.

2. Cut:

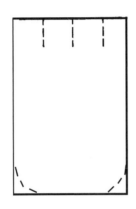 Save corners for ears.

3. Curl the hair. Paste on the ears.

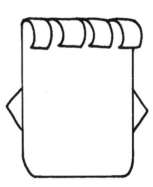

4. Cut out the eyes and a nose.
   Draw a mouth.
   Color the face.

   Examples: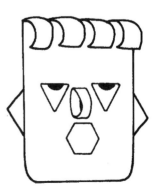

Nombre_____

Haz una lista de 12 animales.

1._____ 7._____

2._____ 8._____

3._____ 9._____

4._____ 10._____

5._____ 11._____

6._____ 12._____

Pon los animales en orden alfabético.

1._____ 7._____

2._____ 8._____

3._____ 9._____

4._____ 10._____

5._____ 11._____

6._____ 12._____

Dibuja tu animal favorito. Haz un círculo alrededor de su nombre en tu lista.

Name_____

List 12 animals.

1. _____ 7. _____

2. _____ 8. _____

3. _____ 9. _____

4. _____ 10. _____

5. _____ 11. _____

6. _____ 12. _____

Put the animals in alphabetical order.

1. _____ 7. _____

2. _____ 8. _____

3. _____ 9. _____

4. _____ 10. _____

5. _____ 11. _____

6. _____ 12. _____

Draw your favorite animal. Circle its name on your list.

Nombre _____

Sigue las instrucciones para hacer una linterna.

1. Recorta el rectángulo.
2. Dóblalo por mitad.
3. Corta las líneas _ _ _ _.

4. Abre el papel.
5. Pega un lado al otro.
6. Añade una cuerda.

dobla

pegadura

Name_____

Follow the directions to make a lantern.

1. Cut out the rectangle.   4. Open the paper.
2. Fold in half on the ___ line.   5. Paste ends together.
3. Cut all _ _ _ lines.   6. Add a string handle.

fold

paste

Nombre _____

Sigue las instrucciones para hacer un payaso.

1. Toma una hoja grande de papel blanco.

2. Haz una cara grande y redonda.
   Traza el contorno de color negro.

3. Pon una nariz roja y chistosa en el centro
   de la cara.

4. Dibuja dos ojos azules y brillantes.

5. Ahora, dale una sonrisa verde y roja.

6. Dale a tu payaso un sombrero verde alto.
   Ponle una flor amarilla y roja.

7. Añade pelo café rizado.

8. Ahora, ponle un corbatín verde con puntos
   amarillos debajo de la barbilla.

Actividad extra: Escribe un cuento sobre el payaso más
chistoso del mundo.

Name_____

Follow the directions to create a clown.

1. Get a large sheet of white paper.

2. Make a big round face. Outline it in black.

3. Make a funny red nose in the middle of the face.

4. Draw two sparkling blue eyes.

5. Now give the clown a cheerful smile. Make it green and red.

6. Give your clown a tall green hat. Put a yellow and red flower on it.

7. Add curly brown hair.

8. Now draw a green bow tie with yellow polka dots under his chin.

Bonus: Write a story about the world's funniest clown.

Haz una lista de 15 cosas que haces en tu casa.

1. _____   6. _____   11. _____

2. _____   7. _____   12. _____

3. _____   8. _____   13. _____

4. _____   9. _____   14. _____

5. _____   10. _____   15. _____

Colorea las palabras para cosas:

en tu recámara - azul

en el cuarto de baño - anaranjado

en la cocina - morado

en la sala - amarillo

Name_____

List 15 things in your house.

1. *a door*

2. *a room*

6. _____

7. _____

11. _____

12. _____

3. _____

4. _____

5. _____

8. _____

9. _____

10. _____

13. _____

14. _____

15. _____

Color the words for things:

    in your room - blue

    in the bathroom - orange

    in the kitchen - purple

    in the living room - yellow

 Beginning Reading Activities • EMC 5305

Un dibujo del otoño

Sigue las instrucciones para completar el dibujo.

1. Haz un hoyo en el tronco con una ardilla asomándose.
2. Traza el contorno del árbol con el color negro.
   Coloréalo de color café.
3. Dibuja un montón de hojas debajo del árbol.
   Coloréalas rojas, anaranjadas y amarillas.
4. Dibuja el Sol y nubes blancas en el cielo.
5. Dibuja un gatito jugando con una hoja anaranjada.
6. Dibuja una bandada de pájaros negros posados en las
   ramas del árbol.
7. Dibújate a tí mismo juntando las hojas.

A Fall Picture

Follow the directions to finish the picture.

1. Make a hole in the tree trunk. Show a squirrel peeking out.

2. Outline the tree with black. Color it brown.

3. Draw a pile of autumn leaves under the tree.
   Color the leaves red, orange, and yellow.

4. Make the Sun and three fluffy clouds in the sky.

5. Make a kitten playing with an orange leaf under the tree.

6. Draw a flock of blackbirds sitting on the branches of the tree.

7. Draw yourself raking the leaves.

Nombre_____

Parte A: Haz una lista de 18 palabras que nombren lugares, trabajos y vehículos.

1. _Hawaii_   7. _____   13. _____

2. _____   8. _____   14. _____

3. _____   9. _____   15. _____

4. _____   10. _____   16. _____

5. _____   11. _____   17. _____

6. _____   12. _____   18. _____

Ahora... intercambia tu lista con un compañero y haz la Parte B.

Parte B: Marca cada palabra en la lista así:

lugares ✔   trabajos ★   vehículos ☺

Escribe tus nombre y el de tu compañero en cada papel.

_____

_____

Name_____

Part A: Make a list of 18 words that name places, jobs, and vehicles.

1. _Hawaii_____   7. _____   13. _____

2. _____   8. _____   14. _____

3. _____   9. _____   15. _____

4. _____   10. _____   16. _____

5. _____   11. _____   17. _____

6. _____   12. _____   18. _____

Now... trade lists with someone and do Part B.

Part B: Mark each word in the list like this:

places ✓   jobs ★   vehicles ☺

Write both of your names on each paper.

_____

_____

Nombre_____

Sigue las instrucciones. Traza el camino con un creyón.

1. Empieza en la entrada. Entra. Dale de comer al elefante.

2. Da una vuelta y camina a la jaula del león.
   Colorea el león de amarillo y café.

3. Voltea a la izquierda y camina más allá del río hasta los osos.
   Colorea el oso grande de café. Colorea el oso pequeño de negro.

4. Camina hasta el corral del rinoceronte.
   Traza el contorno del cuerno con el color negro.

5. Voltea a la derecha y cruza el puente.
   Para. Colorea el agua de azul y el caimán de verde.

6. Camina desde el puente hasta el hipopótamo. Voltea a la izquierda y camina hasta la jaula de la jirafa. Colorea sus manchas.

7. Voltea a la derecha y pasa por el venado y la cebra. Sigue adelante hasta la última jaula. ¿Qué ves allí? _____

Name_____

Follow the directions. Trace your path with a crayon.

1. Start at the entrance. Go inside. Stop to feed the elephant.

2. Turn around and walk to the lion's cage.
   Color the lion yellow and brown.

3. Turn left and walk past the river to the bears.
   Color the large bear brown. Make the small one black.

4. Walk over to the rhino's pen. Outline his horn in black.

5. Turn right and walk over the bridge. Stop and color the water blue
   and the alligator green.

6. Walk from the bridge to the hippo. Turn left and walk to the
   giraffe's cage. Color his spots.

7. Turn to the right and walk past the deer and the zebra. Keep going
   to the last cage. What do you see? _____

Nombre _____

padres	niño	Timoteo
Canadá	alegre	cuello
enojado	EE.UU.	nervioso
pies	pecho	soldado
artista	María	México
sorprendido	emocionado	muñeca
Francia	preocupado	tobillo
brazo	Nueva Zelandia	China

personas	sentimientos	partes del cuerpo	lugares
1. _____	1. _____	1. _____	1. _____
2. _____	2. _____	2. _____	2. _____
3. _____	3. _____	3. _____	3. _____
4. _____	4. _____	4. _____	4. _____
5. _____	5. _____	5. _____	5. _____
6. _____	6. _____	6. _____	6. _____

Escribe una palabra más en cada lista.

7. _____	7. _____	7. _____	7. _____

Name_____

parents	child	Timothy
Canada	happy	neck
angry	U.S.A.	nervous
feet	chest	soldier
artist	Maria	Mexico
surprised	excited	wrist
France	upset	ankle
arm	New Zealand	China

people	feelings	body parts	places
1._____	1._____	1._____	1._____
2._____	2._____	2._____	2._____
3._____	3._____	3._____	3._____
4._____	4._____	4._____	4._____
5._____	5._____	5._____	5._____
6._____	6._____	6._____	6._____

Write one more word on each list.

| 7._____ | 7._____ | 7._____ | 7._____ |

Nombre _____

Marca así: | quién | <u>dónde</u>   (cuándo)

al lado de la cerca   durante la noche

el Halloween pasado   debajo de la mesa

niños alborotados   un granjero cansado

en un frasco   en la lonchera

el payaso chistoso   el abuelito de Rafael

cada día   después de la escuela

enormes jugadores de fútbol mañana muy temprano

en la escuela   una doctora muy ocupada

en mi cabeza   durante mis vacaciones

¿Cuantas palabras hay sobre | quién? | _____

¿Cuantas palabras hay sobre <u>dónde?</u> _____

¿Cuantas palabras hay sobre (cuándo?) _____

Name_____

Mark like this: | who | ~where~   ⬭when⬭

by the fence	during the night
last Halloween	under the table
excited children	a tired farmer
in a jar	in the lunch box
the funny clown	Ralph's grandfather
every day	after school
huge football players	tomorrow morning
around the school	the busy doctor
on my head	on my vacation

How many | who | words? _____

How many ~where~ words? _____

How many ⬭when⬭ words? _____

Beginning Reading Activities • EMC 5305

Nombre _____

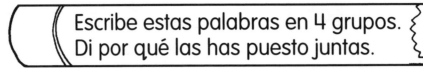
Escribe estas palabras en 4 grupos.
Di por qué las has puesto juntas.

bombones	tío	jugo	agua
primo	chicle	abuelito	gris
pirulí	sobrino	lila	té
morado	rosado	leche	chocolate

Grupo 1: _____   ¿Por qué? _____

_____   _____

_____   _____

_____   _____

Grupo 2: _____   ¿Por qué? _____

_____   _____

_____   _____

_____   _____

Grupo 3: _____   ¿Por qué?_____

_____   _____

_____   _____

_____   _____

Grupo 4: _____   ¿Por qué?_____

_____   _____

_____   _____

_____   _____

Name_____

Put these words into 4 sets.
Tell why you put them together.

jelly beans	uncle	juice	water
cousin	gumdrops	grandpa	gray
lollipop	nephew	lavender	tea
purple	magenta	milk	chocolate

Set 1: _____ Why?_____

_____ _____

_____ _____

_____ _____

Set 2: _____ Why?_____

_____ _____

_____ _____

_____ _____

Set 3: _____ Why?_____

_____ _____

_____ _____

_____ _____

Set 4: _____ Why?_____

_____ _____

_____ _____

_____ _____

Maestro: Cada niño necesitará un papelito cuadrado. 6″ x 6″ (15 x 15cm) es un buen tamaño.

Nombre_____

Sigue las instrucciones para hacer un perro.

1. Empieza con un papel cuadrado.
2. Dóblalo por la mitad de esquina a esquina.

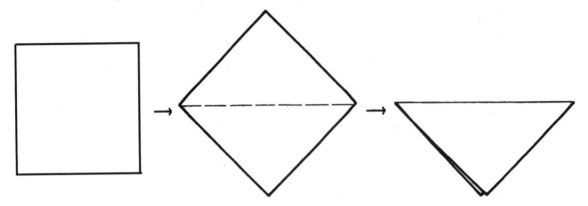

3. Dobla las esquinas hacia abajo para formar las orejas.
4. Dobla una esquina de la parte de abajo para formar la nariz y la boca.

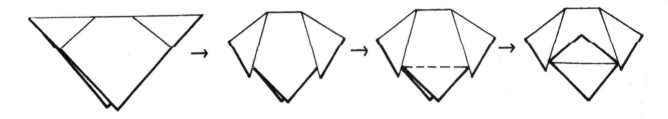

5. Dibújale la cara al perro.

Piensa en un buen nombre para tu nueva mascota.

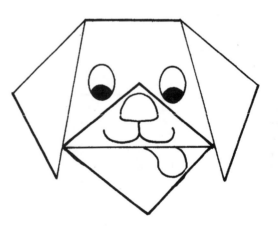

Name_____

Follow the directions to make a dog.

1. Start with a paper square.
2. Fold it in half from corner to corner.

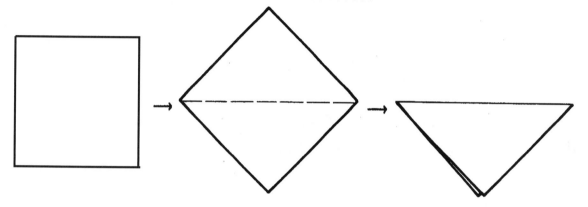

3. Fold down the corners to make the ears.
4. Fold up one part of the bottom to make the nose and mouth.

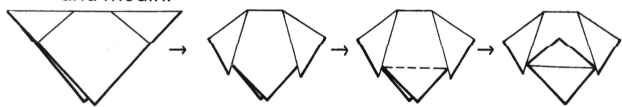

5. Draw a face on the dog.

Think of a good name for your new pet.

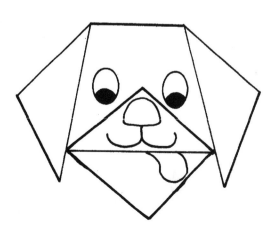

Nombre _____

Sigue las instrucciones para hacer una estrella de mar.

1. Recorta las líneas _ _ _ _ _ _ _.
2. Colorea así:

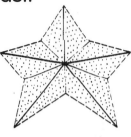
boca arriba

boca abajo

3. Dobla hacia arriba en las líneas _____.
    Dobla hacia abajo en las líneas _____.

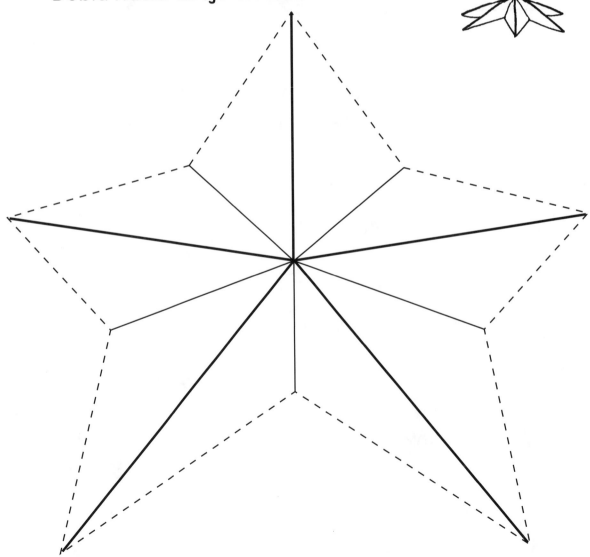

Name_____

Follow the directions to make a sea star.

1. Cut on the _ _ _ _ _ _ lines.
2. Color:

top

bottom

3. Fold up on the _____ lines.
   Fold down on the _____ lines.

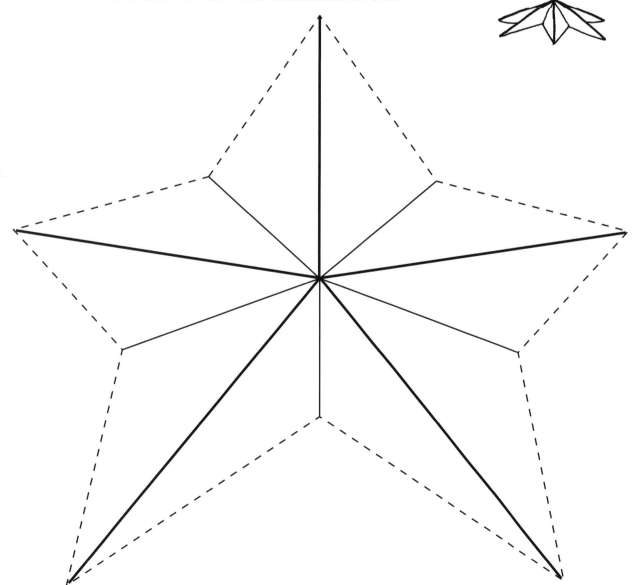

Maestro: Cada niño necesitará un papel periódico o papel de envolver que mide 21" x 21".

Nombre_____

Sigue las instrucciones para hacer un sombrero.

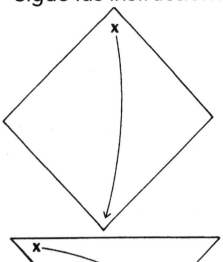

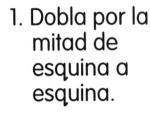

1. Dobla por la mitad de esquina a esquina.

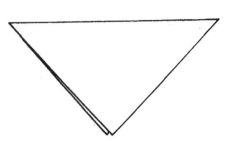

2. Dobla la esquina izquierda hacia el centro del otro lado.

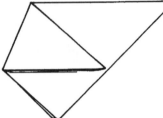

3. Dobla la esquina derecha hacia el centro del otro lado.

4. Dobla una de las partes de abajo hacia arriba.

5. Voltea tu sombrero. Dobla hacia arriba la otra parte de abajo.

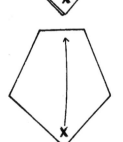

Ahora... póntelo!

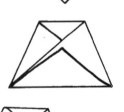

Name_____

Follow the directions to make a hat.

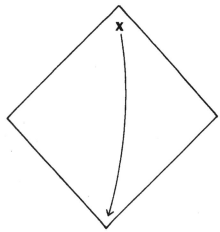
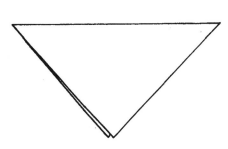

1. Fold corner to corner.

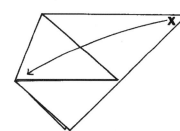
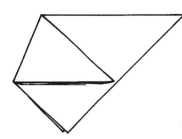

2. Fold left corner to middle of other side.

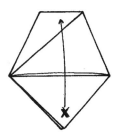

3. Fold right corner to middle of the other side.

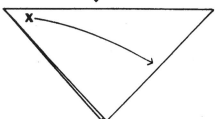
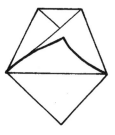

4. Fold one bottom piece up.

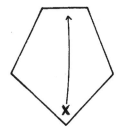
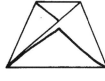

5. Turn your hat over. Fold up the other bottom piece.

Now... wear it!

Secuenciar instrucciones

Esta sección contiene 20 páginas en español que relatan los pasos para desarrollar actividades cotidianas, como por ejemplo ponerse una chaqueta, montar en bicicleta, tender la cama, y otras actividades semejantes. Diez de las actividades incluyen cuatro pasos para secuenciar; las otras diez incluyen seis pasos. Todas las actividades

- están escritas en oraciones sencillas para facilitar la lectura.

- incluyen ilustraciones que facilitan la comprensión de vocabulario nuevo o desconocido.

- siguen el mismo procedimiento: recortar las 4 ó 6 oraciones; arreglarlas de diferentes maneras hasta hallar la secuencia correcta; pegarlas al lado de la ilustración como narrativa.

Después, como trabajo en grupo o independiente, puede animar a los niños a crear sus propias secuencias de instrucciones acompañadas por dibujos que muestren actividades sencillas que saben realizar.

Sequencing Directions

This section contains 20 pages in English that outline the steps for carrying out simple everyday activities such as putting on a jacket, riding a bicycle, making a bed, and other such activities. Ten of the activities include four steps to be sequenced; the other ten include six steps. All of the activities

- are written in simple sentences to support beginning readers.

- include illustrations to support comprehension of new or unfamiliar vocabulary.

- follow the same procedure: children cut out the 4 or 6 sentences, rearrange them until they are correctly sequenced, then paste them alongside the illustration as a simple narrative.

Later, you may wish to encourage children to work in a group or independently to create their own original sequential instructions for carrying out simple everyday activities. Then have them add simple drawings to illustrate their activities.

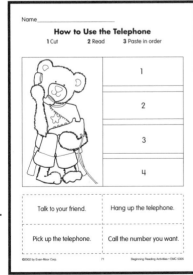

Cómo comer una pizza

1 Recorta   **2** Lee   **3** Pega en orden

	1
	2
	3
	4

Muerde la pizza.	¡Lame tus labios!
Levanta un pedazo.	Corta la pizza en pedazos.

How to Eat a Pizza

1 Cut   **2** Read   **3** Paste in order

	1
	2
	3
	4

Bite into the pizza.	Lick your lips!
Pick up a slice.	Cut the pizza into parts.

Cómo usar el teléfono

1 Recorta   **2** Lee   **3** Pega en orden

	1
	2
	3
	4

Habla con tu amigo.   Cuelga el teléfono

Levanta el teléfono.   Marca el número
que deseas.

Name_____

How to Use the Telephone

1 Cut   **2** Read   **3** Paste in order

1	
2	
3	
4	

Talk to your friend.

Hang up the telephone.

Pick up the telephone.

Call the number you want.

         Beginning Reading Activities • EMC 5305

Nombre_____

Cómo dar de comer al gato

1 Recorta   **2** Lee   **3** Pega en orden

Quita la tapa de la lata.	Llama a tu gato.
Pon la comida del gato en el plato.	Toma una lata de comida para gatos y un plato.

How to Feed the Cat

1 Cut   **2** Read   **3** Paste in order

	1
	2
	3
	4

Take the lid off the can.

Call your cat.

Put the cat food in the dish.

Get a can of cat food and a dish.

Cómo tomar leche

1 Recorta   **2** Lee   **3** Pega en orden

1	
2	
3	
4	

Pon el vaso en el fregadero.	Toma un vaso. Luego, saca leche fría.
Siéntate y bebe la leche.	Llena todo el vaso.

How to Drink Milk

1 Cut   **2** Read   **3** Paste in order

	1
	2
	3
	4

Put the glass in the sink.

Get a glass. Then get out the cold milk.

Sit down and drink the milk.

Fill the glass to the top.

          Beginning Reading Activities • EMC 5305

Cómo jugar con un yo-yo

1 Recorta   **2** Lee   **3** Pega en orden

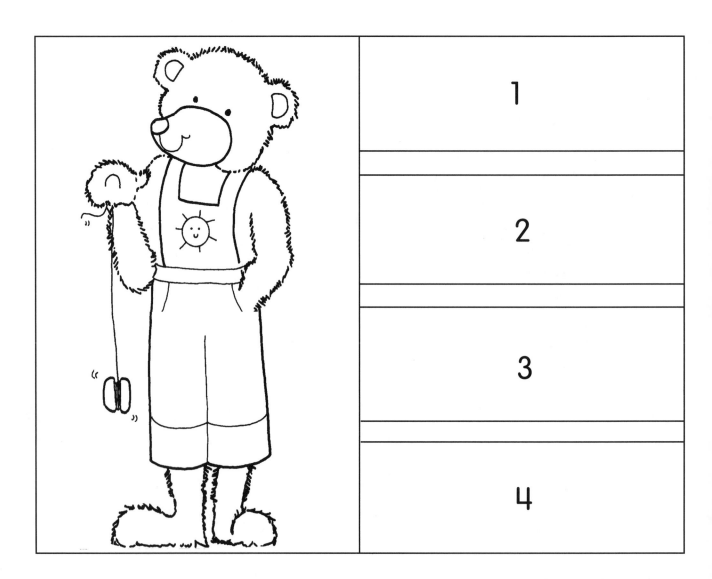

	1
	2
	3
	4

Repítelo muchas veces.

Enrolla la cuerda del yo-yo.

Deja caer al yo-yo y luego hazlo rebotar.

Pon el extremo del hilo en tu dedo.

Name_____

How to Work a Yo-Yo

1 Cut   **2** Read   **3** Paste in order

1
2
3
4

Do this again and again.

Wind the string around the yo-yo.

Drop the yo-yo, then pull it up.

Put the end of the string around your finger.

                   Beginning Reading Activities • EMC 5305

Cómo hacer una máscara

1 Recorta   **2** Lee   **3** Pega en orden

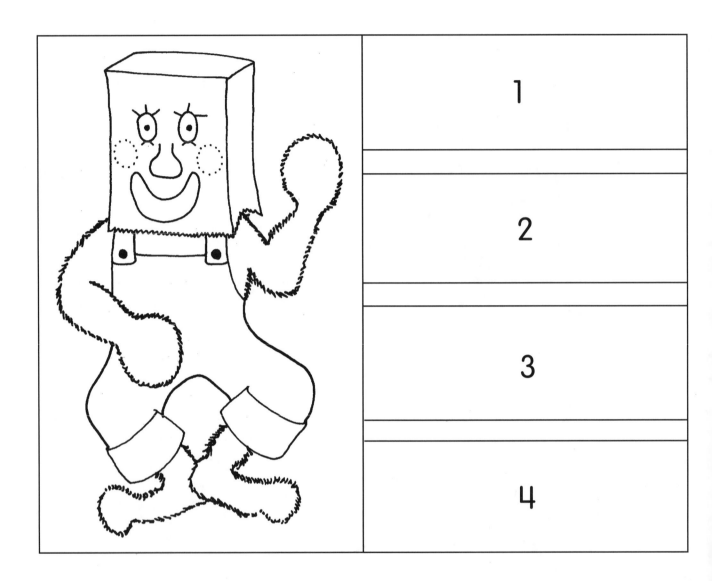

1	
2	
3	
4	

Ponte la máscara y sorprende a un amigo.

Toma una bolsa grande de papel.

Corta dos ojos para que puedas ver.

Ahora, dibuja una nariz y una boca.

How to Make a Mask

1 Cut   **2** Read   **3** Paste in order

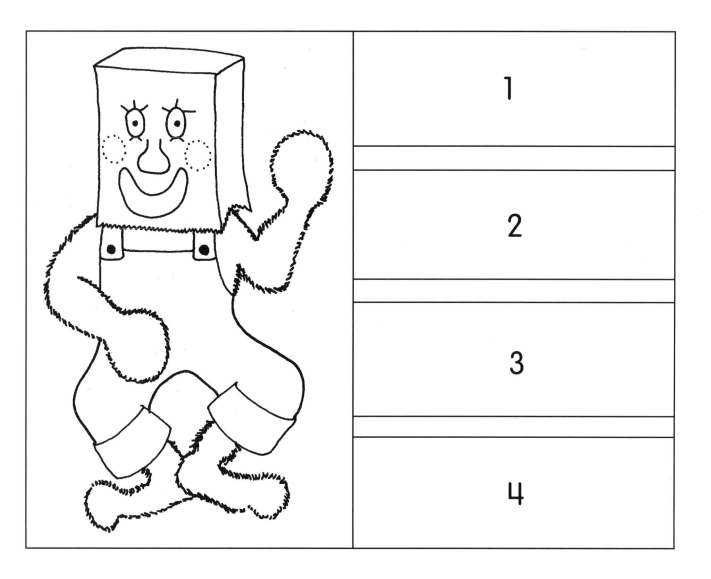

1	
2	
3	
4	

Put on the mask and surprise your pal.	Get a big brown bag.
Cut out two eyes so you can see.	Now draw a nose and a mouth.

Cómo ponerse una chaqueta

1 Recorta **2** Lee **3** Pega en orden

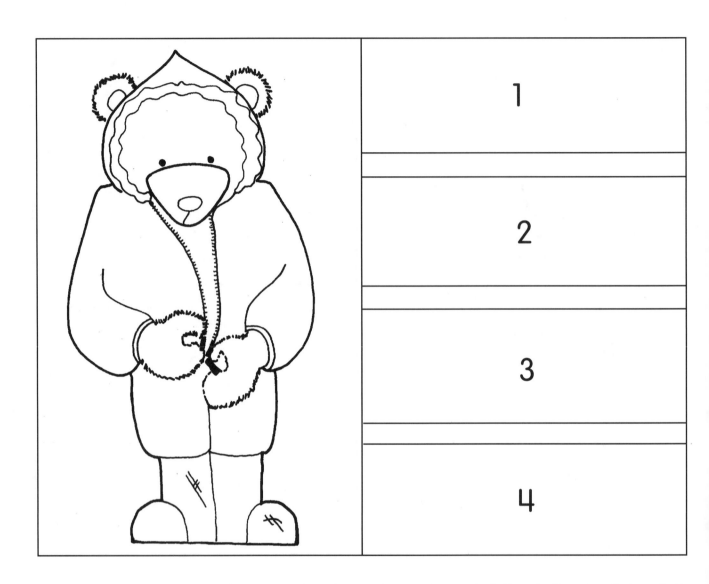

1
2
3
4

Pon tus brazos en las mangas.

Sube el cierre de tu chaqueta.

Hace frío. Toma tu chaqueta.

Ahora puedes ir a jugar afuera.

How to Put on a Jacket

1 Cut   **2** Read   **3** Paste in order

	1
	2
	3
	4

Put your arms in the sleeves.

Zip up your jacket.

It is a cold day. Get your jacket.

Now you can go out to play.

                   Beginning Reading Activities • EMC 5305

Nombre_____

Cómo comer una galleta

1 Recorta   **2** Lee   **3** Pega en orden

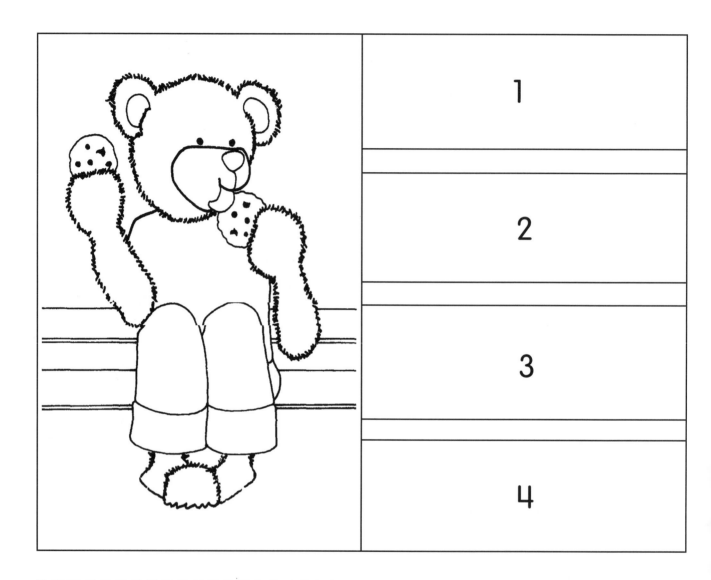

Cómelas a mordidas grandes.	Lleva tus galleas afuera y siéntate en la escalera del patio.
Lámete los dedos.	Toma dos galletas de la caja.

Name_____

How to Eat a Cookie

1 Cut   **2** Read   **3** Paste in order

	1
	2
	3
	4

Take big bites and eat them up.

Take your cookies outside and sit on the back step.

Lick the last bits off your fingers.

Take two cookies out of the box.

Cómo montar a bicicleta

1 Recorta   **2** Lee   **3** Pega en orden

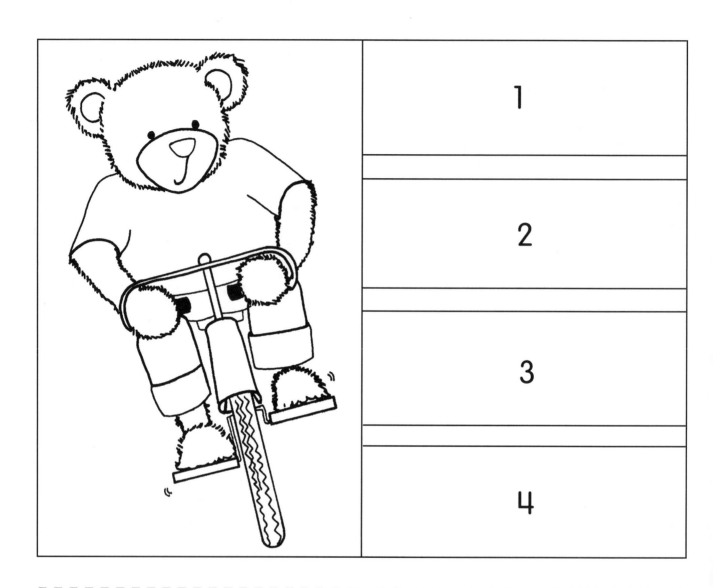

	1
	2
	3
	4

Empuja los pedales para avanzar por la calle.

Usa los frenos para parar.

Súbete a la bicicleta.

Pon tus pies en los pedales y tus manos en el timón.

          Beginning Reading Activities • EMC 5305

Name_____

How to Ride a Bike

1 Cut   **2** Read   **3** Paste in order

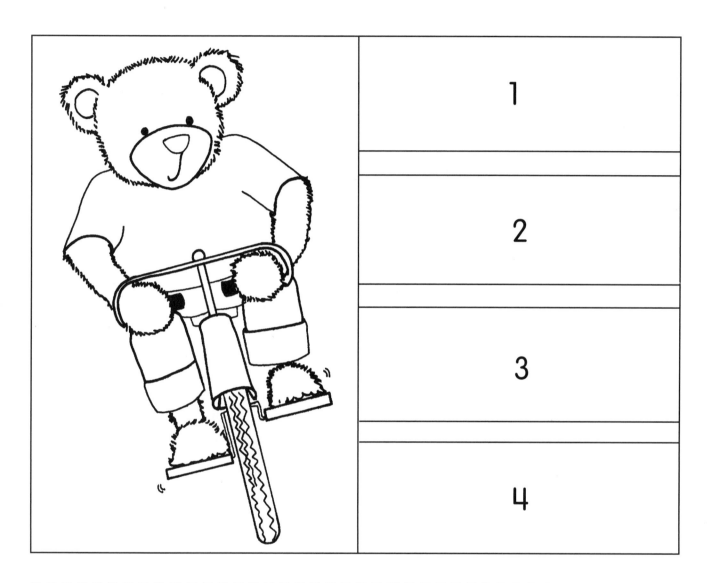

	1
	2
	3
	4

Push the pedals so you can go down the street.	Put on the brakes to stop.
Get on the bike.	Put your feet on the pedals and your hands on the handlebars.

Cómo preparar un helado

1 Recorta   **2** Lee   **3** Pega en orden

	1
	2
	3
	4

Lame el helado y termínalo todo.

Después, saca el helado de la hielera.

Primero, busca una cuchara y un barquillo.

Llena la cuchara con helado y ponlo en el barquillo.

Name_____

How to Make an Ice-Cream Cone

1 Cut   **2** Read   **3** Paste in order

1	
2	
3	
4	

Take a big lick and gobble it down.

Then get the ice cream from the freezer.

First get a scoop and a cone.

Take a big scoop of ice cream and put it on the cone.

Cómo bañar a tu perro

1 Recorta   **2** Lee   **3** Pega en orden

	1
	2
	3
	4
	5
	6

Pon a tu perro en el agua.	Enjuágalo.
Sécalo con una toalla grande y déjalo ir.	Ahora, agarra a tu perro.
Llena un balde con agua y toma una toalla grande.	Lava con jabón a tu perro.

How to Give Your Dog a Bath

1 Cut   **2** Read   **3** Paste in order

	1
	2
	3
	4
	5
	6

Put him in the water.	Wash the suds off the dog.
Dry him with the big towel and let him go.	Now catch your dog.
Fill a tub with water and get a big towel.	Rub the suds all over your dog.

Nombre_____

Cómo pintar una cerca

1 Recorta   **2** Lee   **3** Pega en orden

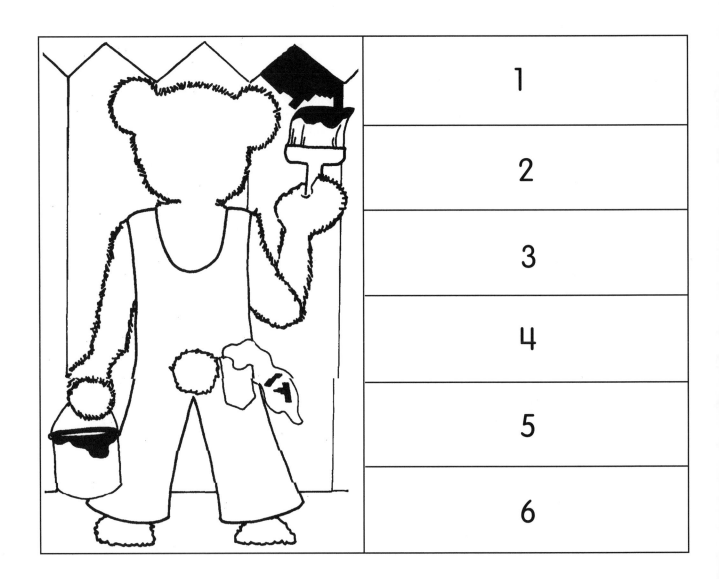

1
2
3
4
5
6

Revisa para ver si quedó alguna parte sin pintar.	Ahora toma una lata de pintura y un cepillo.
Ponte ropa vieja.	Limpia el cepillo y guárdalo.
Quita el polvo de la cerca.	Pinta la cerca.

How to Paint a Fence

1 Cut   **2** Read   **3** Paste in order

	1
	2
	3
	4
	5
	6

Check for any spots you missed.	Now get a can of paint and a brush.
Dress in something old.	Clean the brush and put it away.
Wipe the dirt off the fence.	Brush the paint onto the fence.

Nombre_____

Cómo atrapar a un renacuajo

1 Recorta   **2** Lee   **3** Pega en orden

1	
2	
3	
4	
5	
6	

Perfora la tapa del frasco.	Busca renacuajos en el agua.
Tapa el frasco y lleva los renacuajos a casa.	Busca un frasco en tu casa.
Vete a una laguna.	Agarra algunos renacuajos en tu frasco.

How to Catch a Tadpole

1 Cut   **2** Read   **3** Paste in order

	1
	2
	3
	4
	5
	6

Put holes in the lid.	Look in the water until you see tadpoles.
Put the lid on the jar and take them home.	Find a jar at your house.
Go to a pond.	Scoop up some tadpoles into your jar.

                   Beginning Reading Activities • EMC 5305

Nombre _____

Cómo recoger una manzana

1 Recorta **2** Lee **3** Pega en orden

	1
	2
	3
	4
	5
	6

Toma una bolsa y una escalera.	Lleva la bolsa de manzanas a la casa.
Recoge las manzanas y ponlas en la bolsa.	Bájate de la escalera.
Sube la escalera.	Pon la escalera cerca del árbol.

How to Pick an Apple

1 Cut   **2** Paste   **3** Paste in order

1
2
3
4
5
6

Get a bag and a ladder.	Take the bag of apples into the house.
Pick the apples and put them in the bag.	Go down the ladder.
Go up the ladder.	Put the ladder by the tree.

Nombre_____

Cómo envolver un regalo

1 Recorta   **2** Lee   **3** Pega en orden

| 1 |
| 2 |
| 3 |
| 4 |
| 5 |
| 6 |

Envuelve la caja con papel bonito.	Pon el regalo en una caja.
Ahora tapa la caja.	Amarra la caja con cinta bonita.
Pon una tarjeta debajo de la cinta.	Lleva el regalo a la fiesta.

96

How to Wrap a Gift

1 Cut   **2** Read   **3** Paste in order

	1
	2
	3
	4
	5
	6

Wrap the box in pretty paper.	Set the gift in a box.
Now put on the lid.	Tape a ribbon on the box.
Stick a card under the ribbon.	Take the gift to the party.

97   Beginning Reading Activities • EMC 5305

Cómo tender tu cama

1 Recorta   **2** Lee   **3** Pega en orden

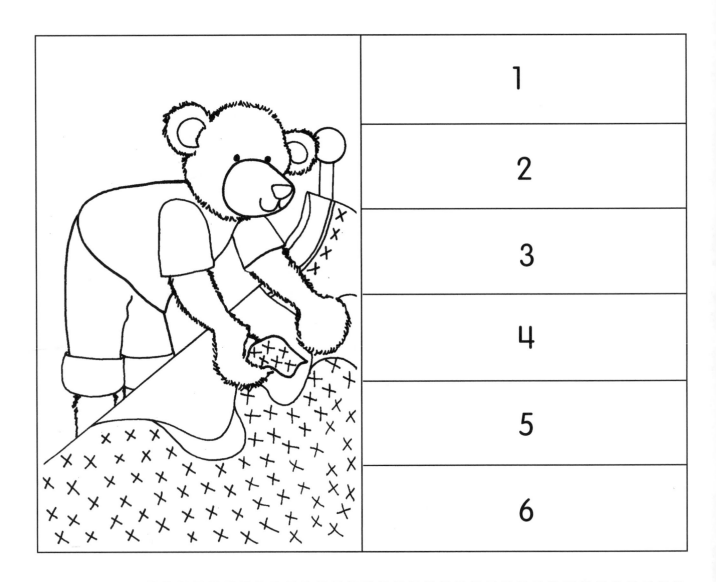

1	
2	
3	
4	
5	
6	

Arregla la cobija.	Acomoda la almohada y ponla sobre la cama.
Pon el cubrecama encima.	Sal de la cama.
Llama a tu mamá para que vea el trabajo que hiciste.	Arregla las sábanas.

Name_____

How to Make Your Bed

1 Cut   **2** Read   **3** Paste in order

	1
	2
	3
	4
	5
	6

Fix the blanket.	Fluff the pillow and set it on the bed.
Put the bedspread on top.	Get out of bed.
Call your mom to see the good job you did.	Pull up the sheets.

         99   Beginning Reading Activities • EMC 5305

Cómo hacer una linterna de calabaza

1 Recorta   **2** Lee   **3** Pega en orden

	1
	2
	3
	4
	5
	6

Hazle ojos, nariz y boca.	Escoge una calabaza anaranjada grande.
Ponla en la ventana	Pon una vela en tu linterna.
Córtale la parte de arriba.	Sácale todas las semillas.

       Beginning Reading Activities • EMC 5305

How to Make a Jack-o'-lantern

1 Cut   **2** Read   **3** Paste in order

	1
	2
	3
	4
	5
	6

Cut out eyes, nose, and a mouth.	Pick a big orange pumpkin.
Set it in the window.	Put a candle in the jack-o'-lantern.
Cut off the top.	Take out all the seeds.

Nombre_____

Cómo tomar un baño

1 Recorta   **2** Lee   **3** Pega en orden

1	
2	
3	
4	
5	
6	

Echa espuma de baño al agua.

Vístete.

Sal de la tina y sécate.

Métete a la tina.

Llena la tina con agua.

Lávate con un paño y jabón.

How to Take a Bath

1 Cut   **2** Read   **3** Paste in place

	1
	2
	3
	4
	5
	6

Add bubble bath.	Get dressed.
Get out of the tub and dry off.	Get into the tub.
Fill the tub with water.	Wash with soap and a rag.

Cómo hacer un bocadillo

1 Recorta   **2** Lee   **3** Pega en orden

	1
	2
	3
	4
	5
	6

Corta el bocadillo por la mitad.	Abre el frasco de crema de cacahuate.
¡Cómetelo!	Saca el pan, la crema de cacahuate y un cuchillo.
Siéntate y dale una gran mordida.	Pon bastante crema de cacahuate en el pan.

Name_____

How to Make a Sandwich

1 Cut   **2** Read   **3** Paste in order

	1
	2
	3
	4
	5
	6

Cut the sandwich in two.	Open the jar of peanut butter.
Eat it up!	Get out the bread, peanut butter, and a knife.
Sit down and take a big bite.	Put lots of peanut butter on the bread.

Cómo sembrar una semilla

1 Recorta   **2** Lee   **3** Pega en orden

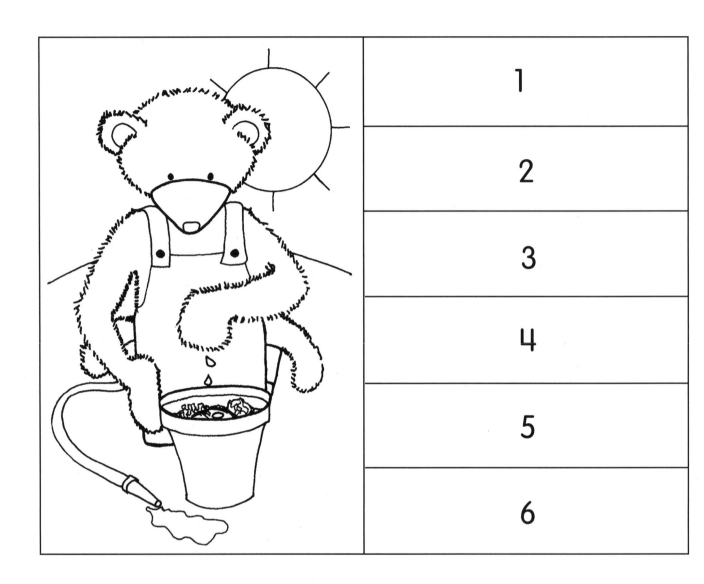

	1
	2
	3
	4
	5
	6

Riega con agua las semillas.	Escoge las semillas que quieres sembrar.
Cubre el hoyo con tierra.	Ahora las semillas podrán crecer.
Luego, abre un hoyo en la tierra.	Deja caer las semillas en el hoyo.

How to Plant a Seed

1 Cut   **2** Read   **3** Paste in order

	1
	2
	3
	4
	5
	6

Water the seeds.	Pick out the seeds you want to plant.
Fill the hole with dirt and pat it down.	Now the seeds can grow.
Next you must dig a hole in the dirt.	Drop the seeds into the hole.

Dibuja . . . luego, escribe

Esta sección contiene 32 páginas en español con instrucciones presentadas en dibujos y palabras. Los niños siguen las instrucciones visuales y escritas para hacer un dibujo, y luego escriben sobre el dibujo que han hecho. Las actividades progresan en dificultad de la siguiente manera:

- En las actividades en las páginas pares de 110–126, los niños siguen las instrucciones para hacer el dibujo y luego responden a preguntas sobre su dibujo (¿Quién o qué? ¿Qué hizo? ¿Dónde? ¿Cuándo? ¿Por qué?).

- En las actividades en las páginas pares de 128–144, los niños siguen las instrucciones para hacer el dibujo y luego escriben tres oraciones sobre lo que han dibujado.

- En las actividades en las páginas pares de 146–168, los niños siguen las instrucciones para hacer el dibujo y luego escribir un cuento corto para acompañarlo.

De esta manera, los niños reciben apoyo para avanzar independientemente en su escritura creativa. Las sugerencias que aparecen en cada página ayudarán a los niños que tienen dificultad en desarrollar la escritura creativa.

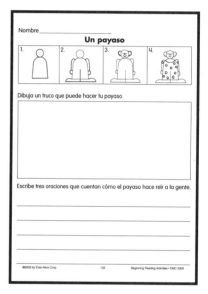

Draw . . . Then Write

This section contains 32 pages in English with directions presented in pictures and words. Children follow the graphic and written directions to make a drawing, then write about the picture they have made. The activities progress in difficulty as follows:

- In the activities on odd pages 111–127, children follow the directions for drawing a picture and then answer questions about the drawing (Who or what? Did what? Where? When? Why?).

- In the activities on odd pages 129–145, children follow the directions for drawing a picture and then write three sentences about their picture.

- In the activities on odd pages 147–169, children follow the directions for drawing a picture and then write a short story about their drawing.

Through this scaffolded process, children receive the support that allows them to progress independently in their creative writing. Writing prompts on each page help children who have difficulty developing their creative writing.

El pato

1.	2.	3.	4.

Dibuja:

Añade:

una laguna

patitos
nadando

hierba
verde

Escribe:

¿Quién o qué? _____

¿Qué hizo? _____

¿Dónde? _____

¿Cuándo? _____

¿Por qué? _____

Name_____

A Duck

1.	2.	3.	4.

Draw:

Add:

a pond

baby ducks
swimming

green grass

Write:

Who or what? _____

Did what? _____

Where? _____

When? _____

Why? _____

El hipopótamo

1.

2.

3.

4.

Dibuja:

Añade:

un río

un pajarito en la espalda del hipopótamo

un sol caliente en el cielo

Escribe:

¿Quién o qué? _____

¿Qué hizo? _____

¿Dónde? _____

¿Cuándo? _____

¿Por qué? _____

Name_____

A Hippo

1.	2.	3.	4.

Draw:

Add:

a river

a little bird on
the hippo's back

a hot sun in the sky

Write:

Who or what?   _____

Did what?   _____

Where?   _____

When?   _____

Why?   _____

El ratoncito

1.	2.	3.	4.

Dibuja:

Añade:

un gran trozo
de queso

un hoyo seguro
para el ratoncito

un gato
hambriento

Escribe:

¿Quién o qué? _____

¿Qué hizo? _____

¿Dónde? _____

¿Cuándo? _____

¿Por qué? _____

A Mouse

1.	2.	3.	4.

Draw:

Add:

a big hunk of cheese

a safe mouse hole

a hungry cat

Write:

Who or what? _____

Did what? _____

Where? _____

When? _____

Why? _____

Un submarino

1.	2.	3.	4.

Dibuja:

Añade:

el mar

plantas que
crecen
en aguas
profundas

uno o más
animales marinos

Escribe:

¿Quién o qué? _____

¿Qué hizo? _____

¿Dónde? _____

¿Cuándo? _____

¿Por qué? _____

Name_____

A Submarine

1.	2.	3.	4.

Draw:

Add:

the sea

deep-water plants

one or more sea animals

Write:

Who or what? _____

Did what? _____

Where? _____

When? _____

Why? _____

El perro

1.	2.	3.	4.

Dibuja:

Añade:

un patio grande

una perrera nueva

un juguete para
tu perro

Escribe:

¿Quién o qué? _____

¿Qué hizo? _____

¿Dónde? _____

¿Cuándo? _____

¿Por qué? _____

Name_____

A Dog

1.	2.	3.	4.

Draw:

Add:

a big backyard

a new doghouse

your dog's toy

Write:

Who or what? _____

Did what? _____

Where? _____

When? _____

Why? _____

Nombre_____

Un coche de carreras

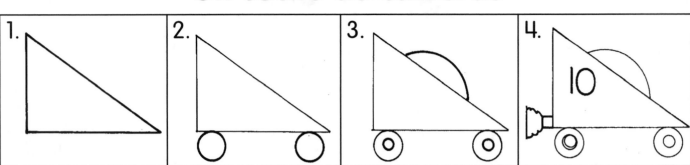

Dibuja:	Añade:
	una pista de carreras
	gente mirando una carrera
	el premio del ganador

Escribe:

¿Quién o qué? _____

¿Qué hizo? _____

¿Dónde? _____

¿Cuándo? _____

¿Por qué? _____

Name_____

A Race Car

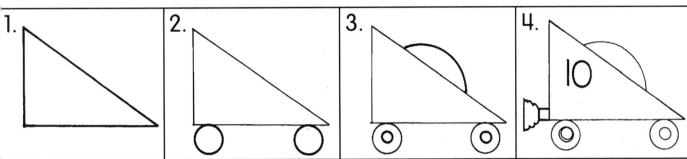

1. 2. 3. 4. **10**

Draw:

Add:

a race track

people
watching a race

the winner's
prize

Write:

Who or what?   _____

Did what?   _____

Where?   _____

When?   _____

Why?   _____

El tiburón

1.	2.	3.	4.
_____			

Dibuja:

Añade:

el mar

un cardumen de peces

algas gigantes

Escribe:

¿Quién o qué? _____

¿Qué hizo? _____

¿Dónde? _____

¿Cuándo? _____

¿Por qué? _____

A Shark

1.	2.	3.	4.
_____			

Draw:

Add:

the ocean

a school of fish

giant seaweed

Write:

Who or what? _____

Did what? _____

Where? _____

When? _____

Why? _____

El conejo

1.	2.	3.	4.

Dibuja:

Añade:

una jaula para tu conejo

algo rico de comer

un plato para el agua

Escribe:

¿Quién o qué? _____

¿Qué hizo? _____

¿Dónde? _____

¿Cuándo? _____

¿Por qué? _____

 Beginning Reading Activities • EMC 5305

Name_____

A Rabbit

1.	2.	3.	4.

Draw:

Add:

a big pen for
your pet rabbit

something good
to eat

a water dish

Write:

Who or what? _____

Did what? _____

Where? _____

When? _____

Why? _____

 Beginning Reading Activities • EMC 5305

Nombre_____

El kiwi

1. 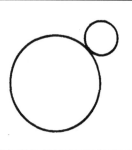	2. 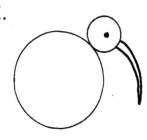	3. 	4. 

Dibuja:

Añade:

unos árboles grandes

un hueco al pie de un árbol para un nido

gusanos o insectos que el kiwi comerá

Escribe:

¿Quién o qué? _____

¿Qué hizo? _____

¿Dónde? _____

¿Cuándo? _____

¿Por qué? _____

A Kiwi

1.

2.

3.

4.

Draw:

Add:

some large trees

a hole under one tree for a nest

worms or insects for the kiwi to eat

Write:

Who or what? _____

Did what? _____

Where? _____

When? _____

Why? _____

El oso

1.	2.	3.	4.

Dibuja tu oso al lado de un río lleno de peces.

Escribe tres oraciones que cuentan cómo el oso va a conseguir su cena.

_____

_____

_____

_____

Name_____

A Bear

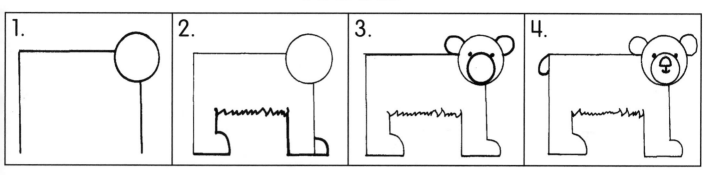

Show your bear by a river full of fish.

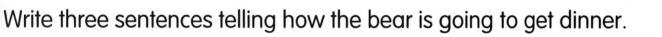

Write three sentences telling how the bear is going to get dinner.

_____

_____

_____

_____

Nombre_____

Un extraterrestre

1.	2.	3.	4.

Dibuja la primera cosa que el extraterrestre vió en la Tierra.

Escribe tres oraciones que explican cómo el extraterrestre llegó a la Tierr

_____

_____

_____

_____

Name_____

A Space Creature

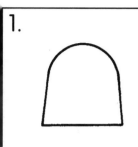 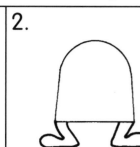  

Show the first thing the space creature saw on Earth.

Write three sentences about how the space creature came to Earth.

Un payaso

1.	2.	3.	4.

Dibuja un truco que puede hacer tu payaso.

Escribe tres oraciones que cuentan cómo el payaso hace reír a la gente.

_____

_____

_____

_____

Name_____

A Clown

| 1.  | 2.  | 3.  | 4.  |

Show a trick your clown can do.

Write three sentences telling how the clown makes people laugh.

_____

_____

_____

_____

Una grabadora

1.	2.	3.	4.

Dibuja cómo te gusta usar tu grabadora.

Escribe tres oraciones que cuentan cómo ganaste suficiente dinero para comprar tu grabadora.

_____

_____

_____

_____

A Boom Box

1.	2.	3.	4.

Show how you like to use your boom box.

Write three sentences telling how you earned enough money to buy your boom box.

_____

_____

_____

_____

_____

El puerco espín

1.	2.	3.	4.

Dibuja lo que puede pasar si un animal choca con este pequeño puerco espín.

Escribe tres oracions que explican lo que pasa en tu dibujo.

_____

_____

_____

_____

Name_____

A Porcupine

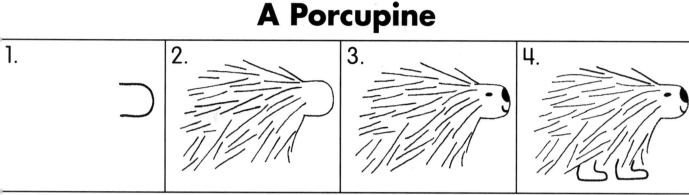

| 1. | 2. | 3. | 4. |

Show what can happen if an animal runs into the little porcupine.

Write three sentences telling what is happening in your picture.

_____

_____

_____

_____

La morsa

1.	2.	3.	4.

Dibuja el mar helado donde vive la morsa.

Escribe tres oraciones que explican lo que hace una morsa hambrienta para conseguir comida.

_____

_____

_____

_____

Name_____

A Walrus

| 1. 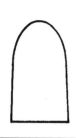 | 2. 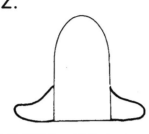 | 3. 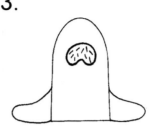 | 4.  |

Show the icy sea where the walrus lives.

Write three sentences about what a hungry walrus does to get food.

_____

_____

_____

_____

La rana

1.	2.	3.	4.

Dibuja un tronco en una laguna donde la rana se puede sentar.

Escribe tres oraciones que explican cómo atrapar a una rana saltarina.

_____

_____

_____

_____

A Frog

1.	2.	3.	4.

Make a log in a pond for the frog to sit on.

Write three sentences telling how to catch a "hoppy" frog.

_____

_____

_____

_____

Un esquimal

1.	2.	3.	4.

Haz un trineo para el niño esquimal.

Escribe tres oraciones que cuentan lo que hace el niño esquimal para divertirse.

_____

_____

_____

_____

An Eskimo

1.	2.	3.	4.

Make a sled for the Eskimo child.

Write three sentences telling what an Eskimo child might do for fun.

_____

_____

_____

_____

Un robot

1.	2.	3.	4.

Dibuja lo que harías si te entregaran un robot en la puerta de tu casa.

Escribe tres oraciones que explican lo que puede hacer tu robot.

_____

_____

_____

_____

Name_____

A Robot

1.	2.	3.	4.
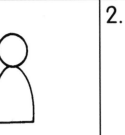			

Show what you would do if a robot was delivered to your door.

Write three sentences telling what your robot can do.

_____

_____

_____

_____

El león

Dibuja el león rugiendo.

Escribe tres oraciones que explican por qué está rugiendo el león.

_____

_____

_____

_____

Name_____

A Lion

Show the lion roaring.

Write three sentences telling why the lion is roaring.

_____

_____

_____

_____

_____

Nombre_____

El mono

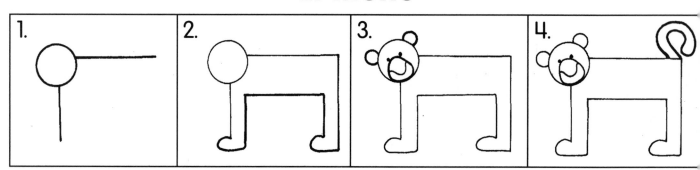

Dibuja al mono parado en un platanal.

Escribe tres oraciones que cuentan lo que el mono va a hacer.

_____

_____

_____

_____

 Beginning Reading Activities • EMC 5305

A Monkey

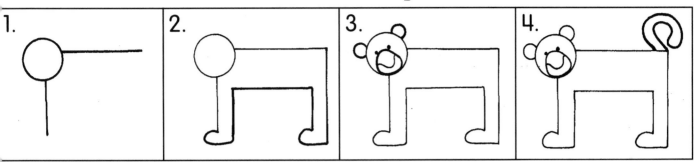

Show the monkey standing under a banana tree.

Write three sentences telling what the monkey is going to do.

_____

_____

_____

_____

Nombre_____

El gato

1.

2.

3.

4.

Dibuja el gato con su juguete favorito.

Escribe tres oraciones que cuentan quién le regaló el juguete al gato.

_____

_____

_____

_____

Name _____

A Cat

1.	2.	3.	4.

Show the cat with its favorite toy.

Write three sentences telling who gave the cat this toy.

_____

_____

_____

_____

El zorro

1.	2.	3.	4.

Dibuja el zorro en frente de la entrada a su madriguera.

Escribe tres oraciones que cuentan lo que el zorro tiene dentro de su madriguera.

_____

_____

_____

_____

Name_____

A Fox

1.	2.	3.	4.
	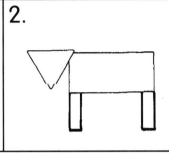	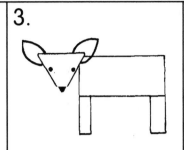	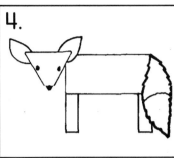

Show the fox in front of its den.

Write three sentences telling what the fox has inside its den.

_____

_____

_____

_____

El pulpo

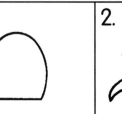   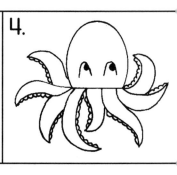

Dibuja el pulpo agarrando algo en sus ventosas.

Escribe tres oraciones sobre lo que el pulpo hará ahora.

_____

_____

_____

_____

Name_____

An Octopus

1.	2.	3.	4.
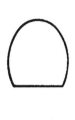		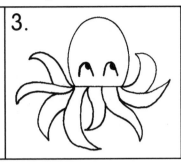	

Show the octopus holding something in its tentacles.

Write three sentences describing what the octopus will do now.

_____

_____

_____

_____

El koala

1.	2.	3.	4.
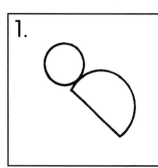		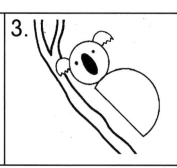	

Dibuja la koala mamá con su cachorro a cuestas.

Escribe tres oraciones que explican a dónde van los koalas.

_____

_____

_____

_____

Name_____

A Koala

1.	2.	3.	4.
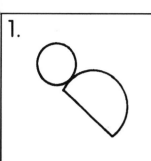		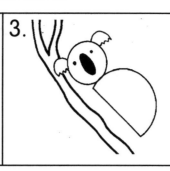	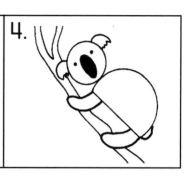

Show the koala carrying her baby on her back.

Write three sentences that tell where the koalas are going.

_____

_____

_____

_____

_____

La nutria

Dibuja un pez nadando cerca de la nutria.

Escribe tres oraciones que cuentan cómo juega la nutria.

_____

_____

_____

_____

Name_____

An Otter

Show fish swimming near the otter.

Write three sentences describing how the otter plays.

_____

_____

_____

_____

El avión

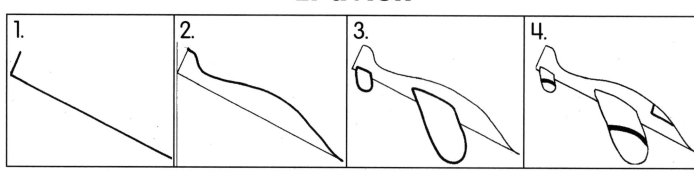

Dibuja el avión volando alto en el cielo.

Escribe tres frases que explican a dónde va el avión.

Name_____

A Jet

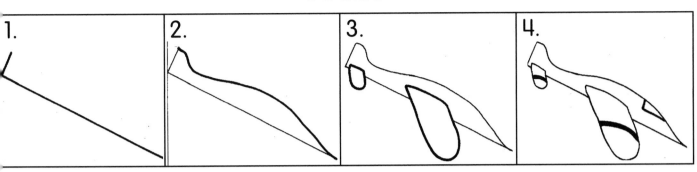

Show the jet flying high in the sky.

Write three sentences describing where the jet is going.

_____

_____

_____

_____

El unicornio

1. 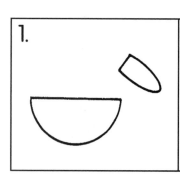	2. 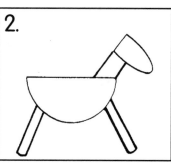	3. 	4. 

Dibuja el unicornio corriendo por un campo florido.

Escribe tres oraciones que explican dónde vive el unicornio.

_____

_____

_____

_____

Name_____

A Unicorn

1.	2.	3.	4.
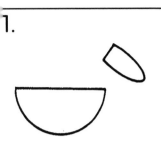	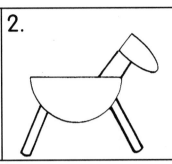		

Show the unicorn running across a field of wildflowers.

Write three sentences describing where the unicorn lives.

_____

_____

_____

_____

Nombre_____

Un jugador de béisbol

| 1. 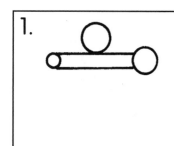 | 2.  | 3. 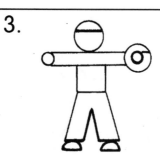 | 4.  |

Dibuja el jugador en segunda base.

Escribe tres oraciones que describen lo que el jugador va a hacer ahor[a]

_____

_____

_____

_____

Name_____

A Ball Player

| 1. 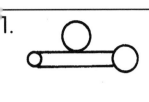 | 2.  | 3. 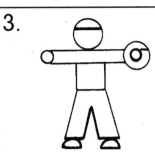 | 4.  |

Show the ball player at second base.

Write three sentences describing what the ball player will do now.

_____

_____

_____

_____

Nombre_____

El dragón

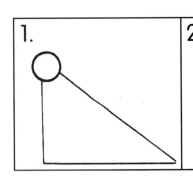 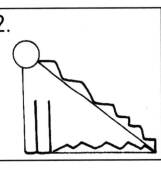 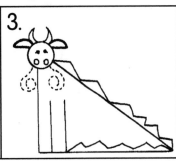 

Dibuja el dragón en su cueva.

Escribe tres oraciones que describen la cueva del dragón.

_____

_____

_____

_____

Name_____

A Dragon

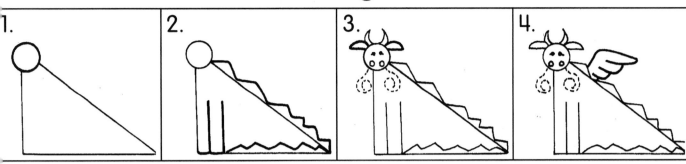

Show the dragon inside its cave.

Write three sentences describing the dragon's cave.

_____

_____

_____

_____

Un helicóptero

1.	2.	3.	4.

Dibuja el helicóptero volando sobre un bosque.

Escribe tres oraciones que cuentan a dónde va el helicóptero.

_____

_____

_____

_____

A Helicopter

1.	2.	3.	4.
		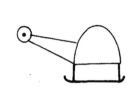	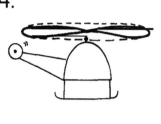

Show the helicopter flying over a forest.

Write three sentences telling where the helicopter is going.

_____

_____

_____

_____

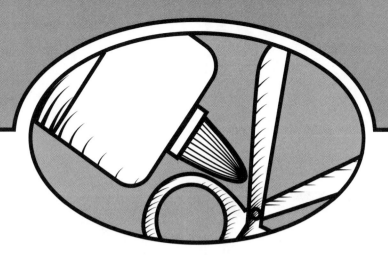

Lee, piensa, corta y pega

Esta sección contiene 20 páginas en español con actividades para practicar destrezas de lectura que incluyen:

- comprensión de lectura
- usar pistas visuales y claves de contexto
- poner en secuencia los acontecimientos de una narración

Read, Think, Cut & Paste

This section contains 20 pages in English with activities that provide practice in the following reading skills:

- reading for meaning
- using visual and context clues
- sequencing events in a story

Al otro lado, escribe y dibuja: ¿Qué hizo la rana en el agua?

Una rana verde está sobre el tronco.

Esta es una laguna grande.

Salta al agua, rana.

Hay un tronco en la laguna.

Name _____

On the back, write and draw: What did the frog do in the water?

A green frog is on the log.

This is a big pond.

Jump into the water, frog.

A log is in the pond.

Al otro lado, escribe y dibuja: ¿Cómo se ve Puerquito ahora?

"Te va a gustar. No intentes escapar."	"¿No es divertido el baño, Puerquito? ¡Qué bién te verás!"
"¡Cuidado! Mira cómo has regado el agua."	"Ven aquí, Puerquito. Es la hora de tu baño."

Name _____

On the back, write and draw: What does Chipper look like now?

"You will like it. Do
not try to get away."

"Isn't this fun, Chipper?
How nice you will look."

"Look out! What a mess
you have made."

"Come here, Chipper. It
is time for your bath."

Nombre_____

Al otro lado, escribe y dibuja: ¿Cómo llegó el hueso a estar bajo la tierra?

¡Qué hueso tan grande encontró! ¡Qué rico! ¡Qué rico!

Susi comió un buen almuerzo. Ahora va a descansar.

Susi comienza a escarbar. La tierra vuela a todas partes.

Susi huele algo rico.

Name _____

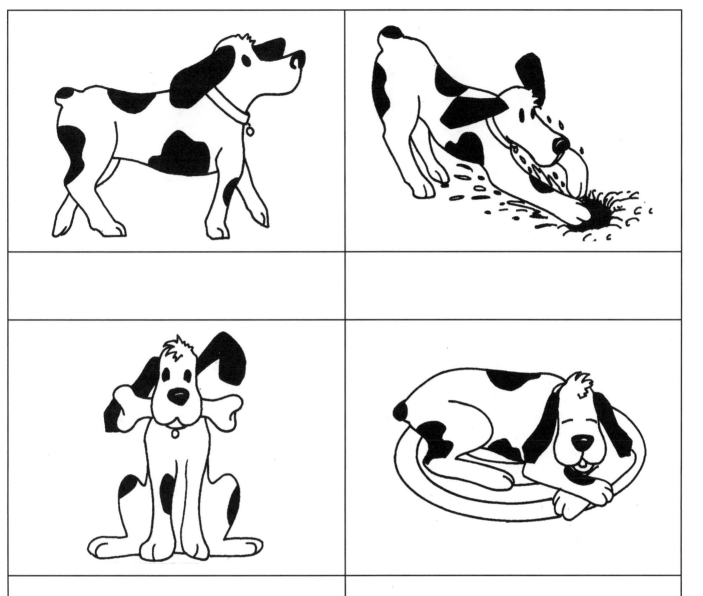

On the back, write and draw: How did the bone get underground?

What a big bone he found. Yum, yum, yum.	Sid had a good lunch. Now he will rest.
Sid began to dig. Dirt went all over.	Sniff, sniff, sniff. Sid smelled something good.

Nombre_____

Al otro lado, escribe y dibuja: ¿A qué van a jugar la tortuga y sus amiguitos?

| Juego con mis amigos. | Vivo cerca de una laguna. |
| Me meto debajo del agua para comer. | Nado todo el día. |

Name _____

On the back, write and draw: What will turtle and his friends play?

I play with my friends.

I live by a pond.

I duck under the water to eat.

I swim around all day.

Nombre_____

Al otro lado, escribe y dibuja: ¿Qué hará Coco ahora?

Se sienta en un lugar soleado y menea su cola.

Ve un pájaro pasar volando.

Coco es una perra feliz. Tiene un patio grande donde puede jugar.

Persigue a una mariposa por todo el patio.

Name _____

On the back, write and draw: What will Coco do now?

She sits in a sunny spot and wags her tail.

She sees a bird go by.

Coco is a happy dog. She has a big yard to play in.

She runs across the yard after a butterfly.

181   Beginning Reading Activities • EMC 5305

Al otro lado, escribe y dibuja: ¿Qué trabajo puede hacer Kiwi?

Kiwi no consiguió el trabajo.
Se fue triste.

"Quiero un trabajo. Preguntaré
aquí," dijo Kiwi.

"Quiero trabajar."
"¿Cómo me puede ayudar un kiwi?"
preguntó el Sr. Lara.

"Puedo ayudar de esta
manera," dijo Kiwi.

On the back, write and draw: What job can Kiwi do?

Kiwi did not get the job.
He went away sad.

"I want a job. I will
ask in here," said Kiwi.

"I want a job."
"How can a kiwi help me?"
asked Mr. Green.

"I can help this way,"
said Kiwi.

Al otro lado, escribe y dibuja: ¿A dónde ha ido el Sr. Panda?

"¿Qué está comiendo, Sr. Oso?"
"¡Yo NO soy un oso!"

"Hola, Sr. Oso."
"No soy un oso."

"¡Oh! No lo sabía y ya se fue el Sr. Panda."

"¿Por qué se va, Sr. Oso?"
"¡No soy un OSO! ¡Soy un panda!"

Name _____

On the back, write and draw: Where has Mr. Panda gone?

"What are you eating,
Mr. Bear?"
"I am NOT a bear!"

"Hello, Mr. Bear."
"I am not a bear."

"Oh! I did not know, and now
Mr. Panda has gone away."

"Why are you running away,
Mr. Bear?"
"I'm not a BEAR! I'm a panda!"

Al otro lado, escribe y dibuja: ¿Qué compró Doña Pata?

"Ahora puedo salir de compras," dijo Doña Pata.

"Quiero salir, pero debo hacer mis quehaceres primero."

Doña Pata arregló su cama rápidamente.

También lavó los trastes.

On the back, write and draw: What did Mrs. Wig-Wag buy?

"Now I can go out and shop," said Mrs. Wig-Wag.

"I want to go out, but I must do my chores first."

Mrs. Wig-Wag quickly made her bed.

She did the dishes, too.

Al otro lado, escribe y dibuja: ¿Qué verá Nena al zambullirse?

Ahora puede comer la almeja.

Nena golpea la almeja con una piedra para romper la concha.

A Nena le gusta nadar en el agua.

Puede zambullirse para agarrar una almeja.

Name _____

On the back, write and draw: What will Otto see when he dives?

Now he can eat the clam. | Otto hits the clam with a rock to crack the shell.

Otto likes to swim in the water. | He can dive down to get a clam.

Al otro lado, escribe y dibuja: ¿Qué hizo Chiquita en la casa de su amiga?

"Haré un barquito."
Y así lo hizo.

Llegó a un charco demasiado grande para cruzar.

Chiquita iba a visitar a una amiga.

Chiquita miraba a todos lados.
"Ya sé qué hacer," dijo ella.

Name _____

On the back, write and draw: What did Huggy do at her friend's?

"I will go on a boat." And she did.	She came to a puddle that was too big to cross.
Little Huggy Bug was on her way to visit a friend.	Little Huggy Bug looked around. "I know what to do," she said.

Al otro lado, escribe y dibuja: ¿Cómo puede Camilo cuidar sus dientes?

| Ahora Camilo puede cortar árboles de nuevo. | El dentista arregló el diente. |
| Camilo se sentía mal. Le dolía un diente. | "Vamos al dentista. Él lo arreglará," dijo Mamá. |

Name _____

On the back, write and draw: How can Bud take care of his teeth?

| Now Bud can cut down trees again. | The dentist did fix the tooth. |
| Bud felt bad. His tooth hurt. | "We will go to the dentist. He will fix it," said Mom. |

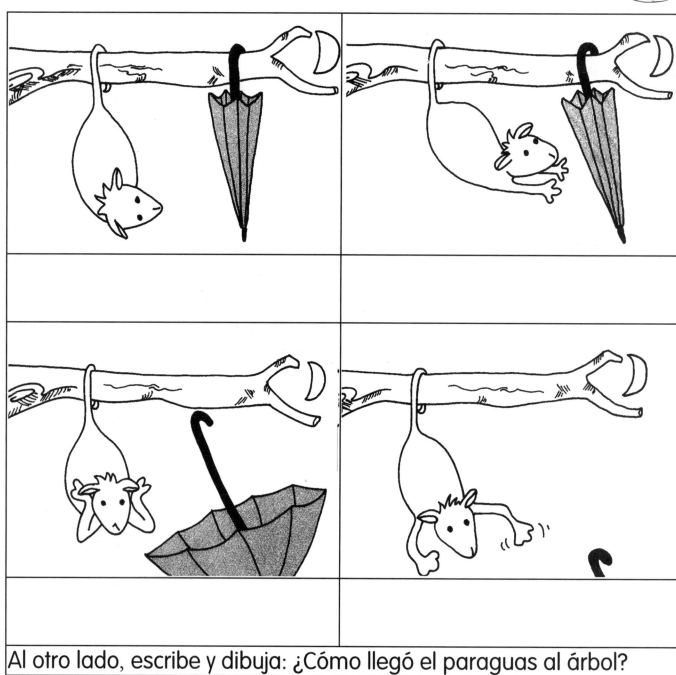

Al otro lado, escribe y dibuja: ¿Cómo llegó el paraguas al árbol?

"Ay, ¿qué he hecho?
¿Sabrá volar?"

"¡Buen viaje! Vuelve a
visitarme algún día."

"¡Despierta! ¡Despierta!
¡Ya oscureció! ¡Levántate!"

"¿Quién eres? ¿Eres nuevo
aquí en el árbol?"

Name _____

and

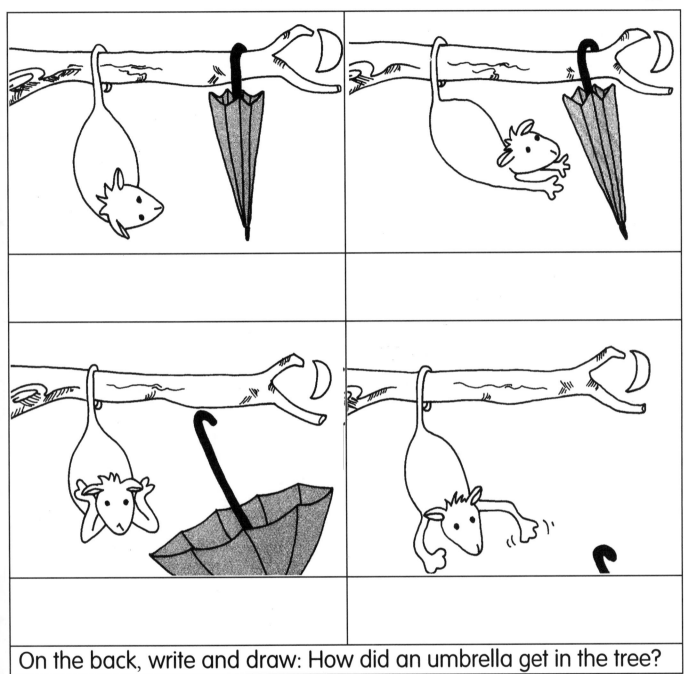

On the back, write and draw: How did an umbrella get in the tree?

©2002 by Evan-Moor Corp.   195   Beginning Reading Activities • EMC 5305

Al otro lado, escribe y dibuja: ¿Cómo pintó las flores el conejo?

"Qué bonitas se ven las flores ahora."

"Los huevos están pintados y aún me sobra pintura."

"Ya sé lo que haré. Pintaré las flores."

"¿Puedes ayudarme, Pájaro? Esto es divertido."

Name _____

On the back, write and draw: How did the rabbit paint the flowers?

"How pretty the flowers
look now."

"The eggs are painted and
I have this paint left."

"I know what I will do.
I will paint the flowers."

"Can you help me, Bird?
It is fun."

Al otro lado, escribe y dibuja: ¿Qué herramientas usó el perro?

"Ahora podemos guardar las herramientas."

¡Pum, pum! "Este es un trabajo difícil."

"¡Qué casa nueva tan bonita!"

"¡Ay, ay! ¡No salpiques la pintura!"

Name _____

On the back, write and draw: What tools did the dog use?

"We can put the tools away now."

Bang, bang, bang. "This is hard work."

"What a pretty new house."

"Oh, oh. Do not splash the paint."

Nombre_____

Al otro lado, escribe y dibuja: ¿Qué truco de magia te gusta más?

"Les presentaré un truco de magia."

"Por favor, dos boletos para la función de magia."

"¡Mira! ¡Qué truco tan gracioso!"

"¿Nos sentamos aquí? Quiero ver todos los trucos."

Name _____

On the back, write and draw: What magic trick do you like best?

"I will do a magic trick for you."

"Two tickets for the magic show, please."

"Oh, look! What a funny trick."

"Can we sit here? I want to see all of the magic show."

Nombre _____

Al otro lado, escribe y dibuja: ¿Cómo salió Gitano de su jaula?

"Allí está Gitano, sobre la pipa de Papá. ¡Vamos a agarrarlo!"

"Ven, Gitano. Hay algo rico aquí."

"Gitano está feliz en su jaula. Oye cómo canta."

"¡Mira! Gitano salió de su jaula."

On the back, write and draw: How did Flash get out of the cage?

"There is Flash on Dad's pipe. Let's catch him!"

"Come here, Flash. Here is something good."

"Flash is happy to be back. He is singing."

"Look! Flash is out of his cage."

Al otro lado, escribe y dibuja: ¿Cómo puede Pescadito agradecer a su amigo?

"Gracias. Eres un buen amigo."

"Mira las lindas conchas. Quisiera tenerlas en mi casa."

"Yo puedo ayudarte, amiguito. Tengo muchos brazos."

"Esto tardará bastante tiempo."

Name _____

On the back, write and draw: How can Fish thank his friend?

"Thank you. You are a good friend."

"Look at these pretty shells. I wish I had them at my house."

"I can help you, little friend. I have many arms."

"This will take a long time."

Al otro lado, escribe y dibuja: ¿Qué harán ellos después del almuerzo?

"Es divertido ir de excursión al parque con los amigos," dijo Ana.

"¿Qué puedo hacer en este día de sol?" preguntó la hormiga Ana.

Ana invita a todos sus amiguitos para ir a almorzar al parque.

"Invita a tus amiguitos a ir de excursión," dijo la Sra. Hormiga.

Name _____

On the back, write and draw: What will they do after lunch?

"It's fun to picnic in the park with friends," laughed Ann.

"What can I do this sunny day?" asked Ann Ant.

So Ann invited all of her friends to a picnic in the park.

"Ask your friends to go on a picnic," said Mrs. Ant.

Nombre_____

Al otro lado, escribe y dibuja: ¿Dónde aterrizará el avión?

Es divertido volar por las nubes.	El avión avanzó por la pista.
Se subió al asiento del piloto.	El piloto caminó hacia su avión.

Name _____

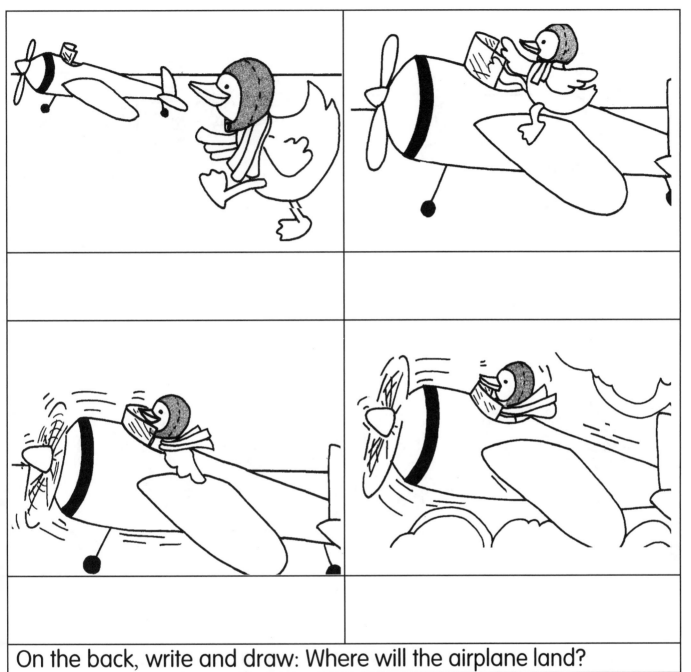

On the back, write and draw: Where will the airplane land?

It is fun to fly in and out of the clouds.

The airplane went down the runway.

He jumped into the cockpit.

The pilot went to his airplane.

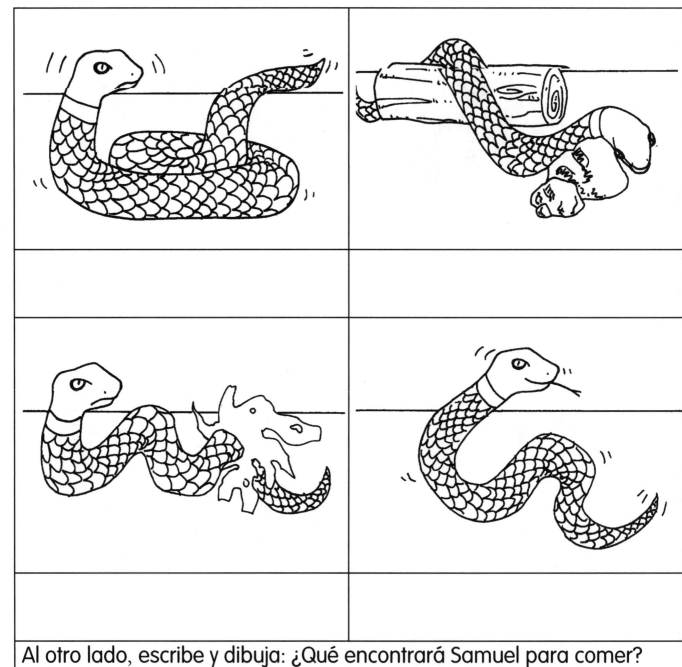

Al otro lado, escribe y dibuja: ¿Qué encontrará Samuel para comer?

Algo le molestaba a la culebra Samuel. Le picaba la piel.

Toda la piel vieja se cayó.

Por fin, Samuel se sintió mejor. Se fue a buscar algo de comer.

Samuel reptaba por las piedras y debajo de los troncos.

Name _____

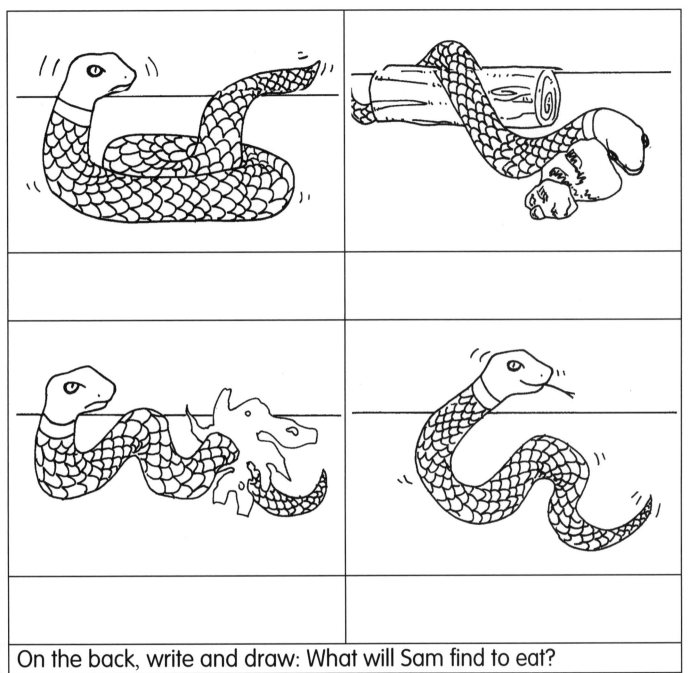

On the back, write and draw: What will Sam find to eat?

Sam C. Snake felt funny.
His skin was "itchy."

All the old skin came off.

Now Sam felt fine. Off he went
to find something to eat.

Sam slithered over rocks and
under logs.

       Beginning Reading Activities • EMC 5305

Conociéndome a mí mismo

Esta sección contiene 24 páginas en español con actividades para ayudar a los niños a desarrollar su autoconcepto y entenderse mejor a sí mismos. Se pueden usar estas páginas de las siguientes maneras:

- Cada página puede utilizarse para experiencias individuales.
- Se pueden engrapar las 24 páginas para hacer libritos individuales.
- Las páginas se pueden emplasticar y usarse para dar inicio a conversaciones en grupo pequeño o con toda la clase.

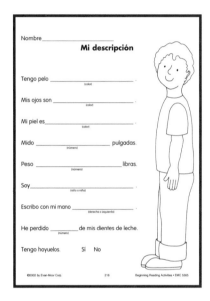

All About Me

This section contains 24 pages in English with activities to help children develop their self-concept and to better understand themselves. These pages may be used in any of the following ways:

- Each page may be used as an individual experience.
- All 24 pages may be stapled together to make individual booklets.
- You may laminate the pages and use each one to spark discussion in small groups or with the whole class.

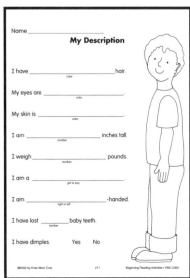

El único

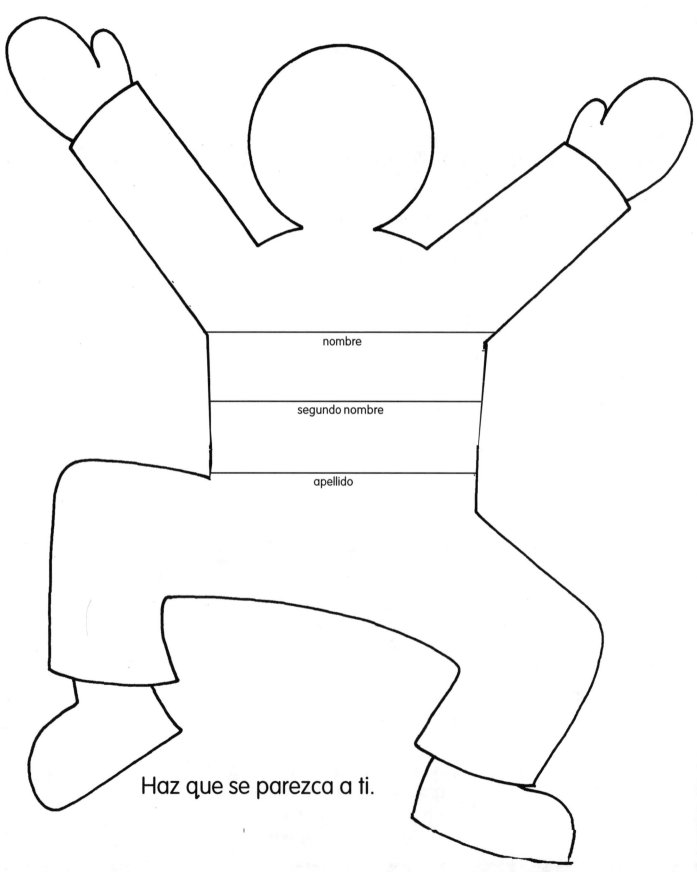

nombre

segundo nombre

apellido

Haz que se parezca a ti.

 Beginning Reading Activities • EMC 5305

Name_____

The One and Only

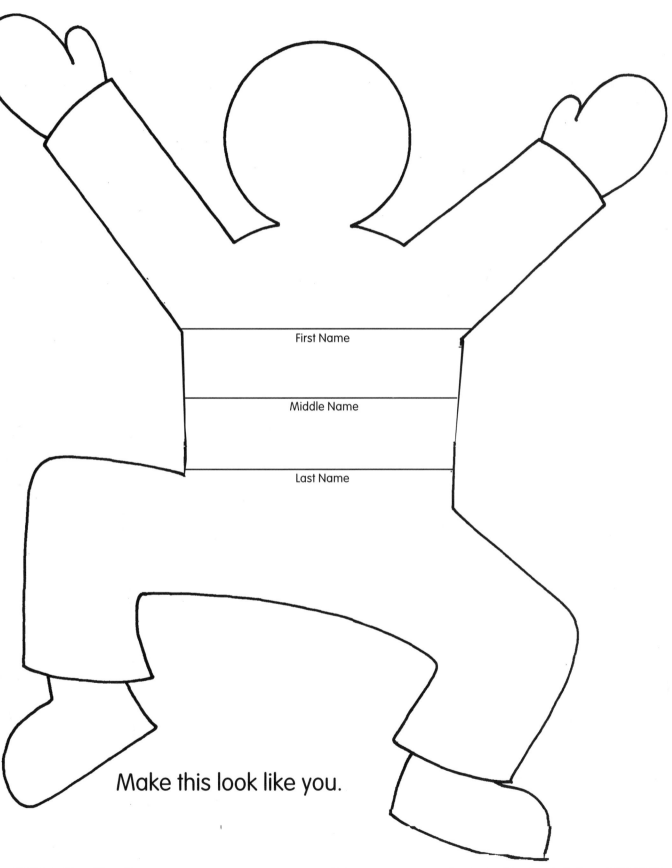

First Name

Middle Name

Last Name

Make this look like you.

Nombre _____

Mi descripción

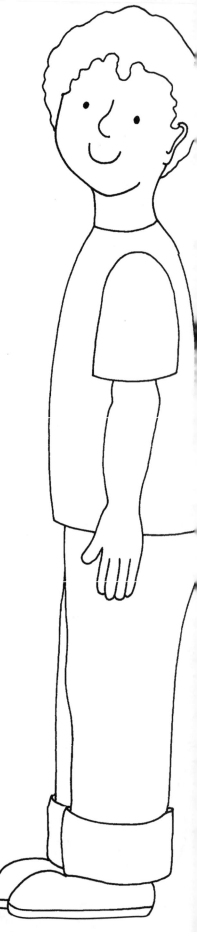

Tengo pelo _____ .
(color)

Mis ojos son _____ .
(color)

Mi piel es_____ .
(color)

Mido _____ pulgadas.
(número)

Peso _____ libras.
(número)

Soy_____ .
(niño o niña)

Escribo con mi mano _____ .
(derecha o izquierda)

He perdido _____ de mis dientes de leche.
(número)

Tengo hoyuelos.   Sí   No

Name_____

My Description

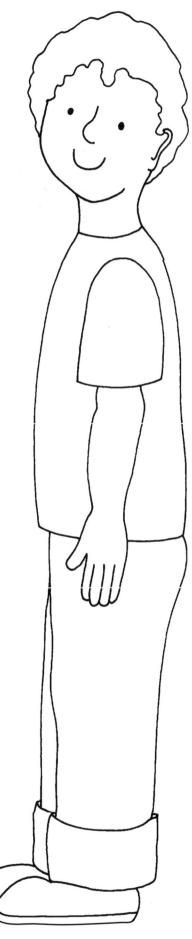

I have _____hair.

color

My eyes are _____.

color

My skin is _____.

color

I am _____ inches tall.

number

I weigh _____ pounds.

number

I am a _____.

girl or boy

I am _____-handed.

right or left

I have lost _____ baby teeth.

number

I have dimples.   Yes   No

Nombre_____

Más datos acerca de mí

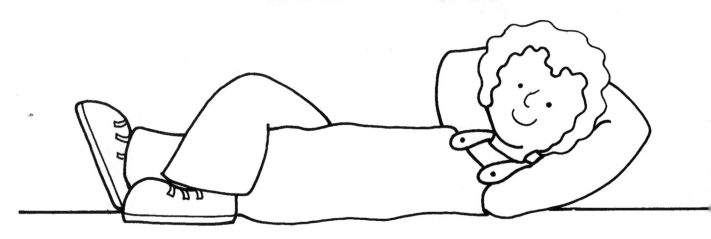

1. Mi nombre completo es _____

2. Tengo _____ años.

3. Nací el día _____ de _____.
   _(número)   _(mes)

4. El número de mi casa es _____

   en la calle _____

   en la ciudad de_____

   en el estado de_____

   en el país de _____

5. Mi número de teléfono es _____

Name_____

More Facts About Me

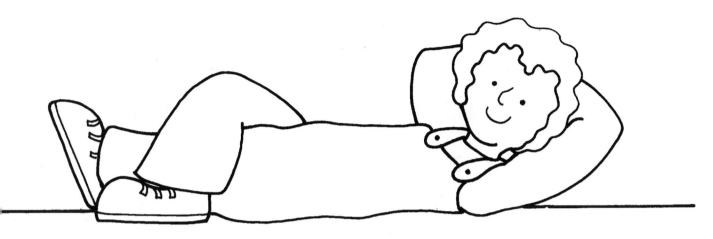

1. My full name is _____

2. My age is _____

3. My birthdate is _____

4. My house number is _____

   on _____
                          (street)

   in the city of _____

   in the state of _____

   in the country of _____

5. My phone number is _____

Nombre_____

Diseña una camiseta especialmente para ti.

1. Pon tus iniciales o tu apodo.

2. Haz un dibujo que muestre lo que te gusta hacer. Usa tus colores favoritos.

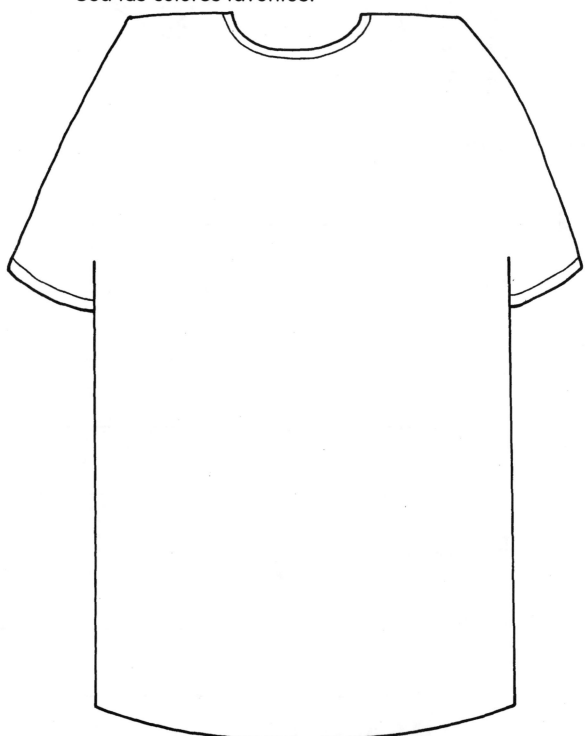

Name_____

Design a T-shirt just for you.

1. Add your initials or nickname.

2. Draw a picture that shows what you like to do.
   Use your favorite colors.

Beginning Reading Activities • EMC 5305

Nombre_____

Las mis huellas de mis pies el día _____

(fecha)

1. Quítate tus zapatos y calcetines.

2. Traza cada pie con cuidado en la caja apropiada.

pie izquierdo	**pie derecho**

My Footprints on _____
date

1. Take off your shoes and socks.

2. Trace each foot carefully in the correct box.

Left foot   **Right foot**

                   Beginning Reading Activities • EMC 5305

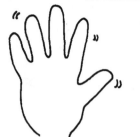

¡Mis huellas digitales son únicas!

1. Traza tus manos.

2. Pon tus huellas digitales al final de cada dedo. (Usa tinta para sellos.)

mano izquierda   **mano derecha**

Name_____

My fingerprints are unique!

1. Trace your hands.

2. Place your fingerprints at the end of each finger.
   (Use a stamp pad.)

Left hand   **Right hand**

225   Beginning Reading Activities • EMC 5305

Nombre_____

Mis talentos y mis sueños

Yo tengo talento en...

1. _____

2. _____

3. _____

Estoy aprendiendo a...

1. _____

2. _____

3. _____

Algún día quisiera poder...

1. _____

2. _____

3. _____

Name_____

My Talents and Dreams

I am already good at...

1. _____

2. _____

3. _____

I'm learning how to...

1. _____

2. _____

3. _____

Someday I hope to be able to...

1. _____

2. _____

3. _____

El apellido de mi familia es _____

A mi familia le gusta hacer muchas cosas juntas. Aquí hay algunas cosas que hacemos.

1. _____

2. _____

3. _____

Mira la familia _____ trabajar juntos.
(apellido)

Mira la familia _____ jugar juntos.
(apellido)

Name_____

My family name is_____

My family likes to do many things together. Here are some things we like to do.

• _____

• _____

• _____

See the _____ family work together.
(last name)

See the _____ family play together.
(last name)

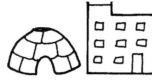 **Donde vivo**

Esta es la casa donde vive la familia _____

Dibuja tu casa.
Haz una ventana por cada persona en tu familia.
Dibuja cada persona en una ventana distinta.
No te olvides de dibujarte a ti mismo.

Name_____

 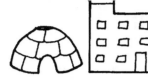 **Where I Live**

This is the house where the_____
family lives.

Draw your house.
Make a window for each person in your family.
Draw each person in a different window.
Don't forget yourself.

Nombre_____

El árbol genealógico de la familia_____

abuelo

abuela

abuelo

abuela

papá

mamá

yo

Mis hermanos y hermanas

_____

_____

Name_____

_____'s **Family Tree**

grandfather

grandmother

grandmother

grandfather

_____
father

_____
mother

_____
me

My brothers and sisters

_____

_____

233

Encuentra la familia

```
p a d r e z h i j a
i a f s o b r i n o
m a d r e r l u h j
o b b c d e f o g h
s o b r i n a r s t
j l n h e r m a n o
c f i j t í a t w p
d e g t k o b l x r
l h n i l h u o y i
h i j o m q e v t m
e z u i n p l i v o
r b f j t í o s w x
m h e r m a n a z y
a c g k m p r u a b
n d h l p a d r e s
a b u e l a c d e f
```

padre
madre
hermana
hermano
padres
primo
sobrino
sobrina
hija
hijo
abuela
abuelo
tía
tío

Find the Family

father
mother
sister
brother
parents
cousin
nephew
niece
daughter
son
grandmother
grandfather
aunt
uncle

s	o	n	a	g	f	p	e	d	s	y	i	d
b	t	s	g	r	c	o	u	s	i	n	j	a
u	p	z	f	a	i	z	e	y	s	f	m	u
c	a	q	u	n	c	l	e	j	t	k	k	g
g	r	a	n	d	m	o	t	h	e	r	x	h
d	e	r	t	f	o	n	h	h	r	l	q	t
v	n	d	o	a	t	e	m	r	w	g	n	e
e	t	q	u	t	h	a	n	h	i	g	w	r
y	s	m	l	h	e	u	e	n	k	l	k	c
f	a	t	h	e	r	n	p	d	f	h	v	b
b	v	g	b	r	o	t	h	e	r	c	c	x
p	w	a	j	t	s	a	e	s	p	m	b	u
n	i	e	c	e	o	n	w	z	r	o	l	a

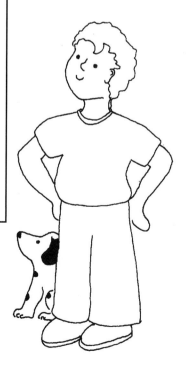

Mis amigos

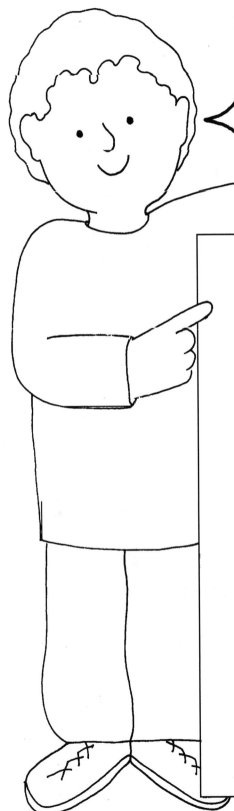

A mí me gustan muchas personas. Algunas de estas personas son especiales para mí. Estas personas son mis amigos.

Aquí están los nobres de algunos de mis amigos.

1. _____

2. _____

3. _____

4. _____

5. _____

6. _____

Name_____

My Friends

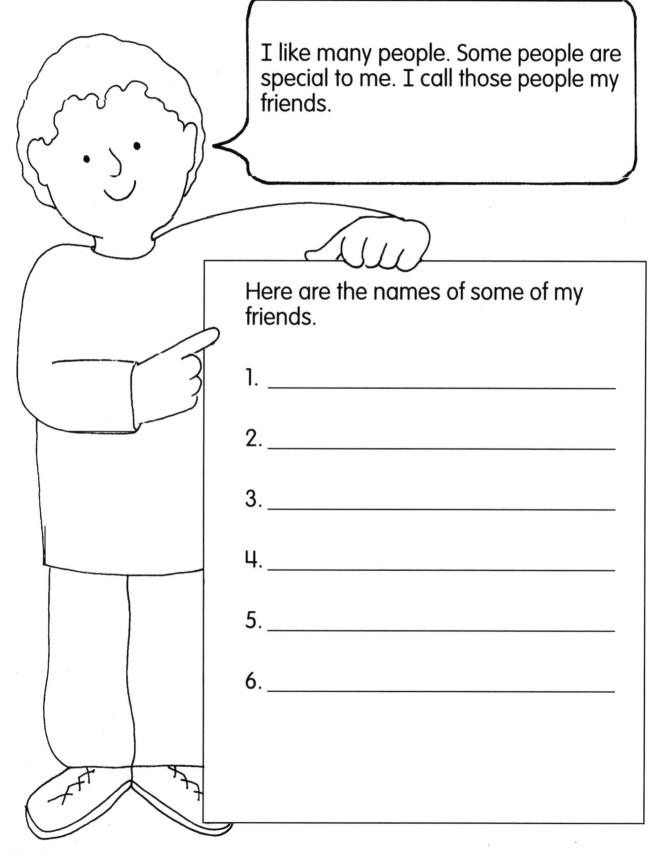

I like many people. Some people are special to me. I call those people my friends.

Here are the names of some of my friends.

1. _____

2. _____

3. _____

4. _____

5. _____

6. _____

☺ ☺ ☺ **Más sobre mis amigos** ☺ ☺ ☺

Dibújate con tus amigos.

A mis amigos y a mí nos gusta

_____

_____

_____

No nos gusta

_____

_____

_____

A veces hago cosas porque mis amigos las hacen, pero la mayoría del tiempo yo decido lo que hago.

Name_____

☺ ☺ ☺ More About My Friends ☺ ☺ ☺

Draw you and your friends.

My friends and I like to

_____

_____

_____

We don't like to

_____

_____

_____

Sometimes I do things because my friends do them, but most of the time I make my own choices.

Las mascotas de _____
(nombre)

Las mascotas que yo tengo son:

_____ _____ _____

Así son mis mascotas:

Para comer, les doy _____ .

Mis mascotas duermen en _____ .

Mis mascotas pueden hacer trucos.   sí   no

Si pudiera tener una nueva mascota, yo quisiera tener _____.

Se vería así:

La llamaría _____ .

_____ 's Pets
(name)

The pets I already have are:

_____   _____   _____

My pets look like this:

feed my pets _____ .

My pets sleep in a _____ .

My pets can do tricks.   yes   no

If I could have a new pet, I would get a _____ .

It would look like this:

would name it _____ .

Nombre_____

Juguetes

Ahora me gusta jugar con

_____.

Tengo muchos juguetes.
Cuando era pequeño, mi juguete favorito era

_____.

Si pudiera tener un nuevo juguete, escogería un

_____.

Puedes encontrar juguetes en lugares chistosos.

Encontré _____en la cocina.

Lo uso para_____.

Encontré _____ en el garaje.

Lo uso para_____.

Encontré _____ en el patio.

Lo uso para _____.

Name_____

Toys

I have many toys. My favorite toy when I was small was

_____.

Now I like to play with

_____.

If I could have a new toy, I would get

_____.

You can find toys in funny places.

I found _____in the kitchen.

I use it to _____.

I found _____in the garage.

I use it to _____.

I found _____ in the yard.

I use it to _____.

Nombre_____

Mis cosas favoritas

1. Mi color favorito es _____ .

2. El programa de tele que me gusta más es_____

_____

3. Las comidas más ricas son _____ ,

_____ , _____ y _____ .

4. Me gusta leer libros sobre _____ .

5. Mi canción favorita es _____ .

6. El deporte que me gusta más es_____ .

7. Me gusta ir a_____ .

en las vacacioes para poder _____ .

 Beginning Reading Activities • EMC 5305

Name_____

My Most Favorite Things

_____

. My favorite color is _____ .

2.The TV show I like the most is _____

_____

3.The best tasting foods are _____ ,

_____ , _____ , and _____ .

4.I like to read books about _____ .

5.My favorite song is _____ .

6.The sport I like best is _____ .

7.I like to go to _____

on my vacation, so that I can _____ .

Nombre_____

Los cosas que me gustan menos

1. No me gusta el color _____ .

   Me hace pensar en _____ .

2. La comida que realmente me disgusta es _____

   porque_____ .

3. El peor programa en la tele es_____ .

4. No me gustan los libros sobre_____ .

5. La canción que me vuelve loco es_____ .

6. El juego que no me gusta jugar es _____ .

7. Nunca iría a_____
   para mis vacaciones.

Name_____

My Least Favorite Things

1. I don't like the color _____.

It makes me think of _____.

2. The food I really hate is _____

because _____.

3. The worst show on TV is_____.

4. I really don't like books about _____.

5. The song that drives me crazy is _____.

6. The game I hate to play is _____.

7. I would never go to _____
on my vacation.

Cuando _____ era pequeño

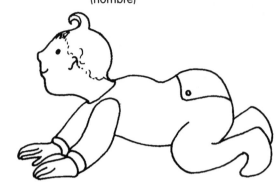

Cuando solamente tenía un año...

No podía

1. _____ .

2. _____ .

3. _____ .

Sí podía

1. _____ .

2. _____ .

3. _____ .

When _____ Was Small
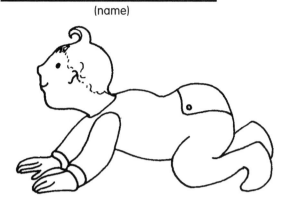

(name)

When I was only one year old...

couldn't

_____ .

_____ .

_____ .

was able to

_____ .

_____ .

_____ .

Cuando _____ sea mayor
(nombre)

Podré

1. _____.

2. _____.

3. _____.

No podré

1. _____.

2. _____.

3. _____.

When _____ Grows Up
(name)

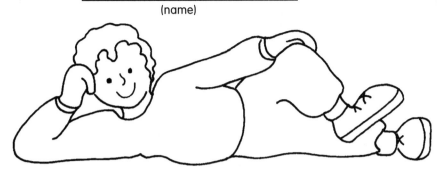

will be able to

_____.

_____.

_____.

won't be able to

_____.

_____.

_____.

Nombre_____

Recuerdo

Lo **mejor** que me ha pasado hasta ahora es...

_____.

_____.

_____.

_____.

Lo **peor** que me ha pasado es...

_____.

_____.

_____.

Name_____

I Remember

The **best** thing that has happened to me so far...

_____ .

_____ .

_____ .

_____ .

The **worst** thing that ever happened to me...

_____ .

_____ .

_____ .

_____ .

Nombre_____

Mis dimensiones

Trabaja con una cinta de medir y un
amigo para tomar estas medidas:

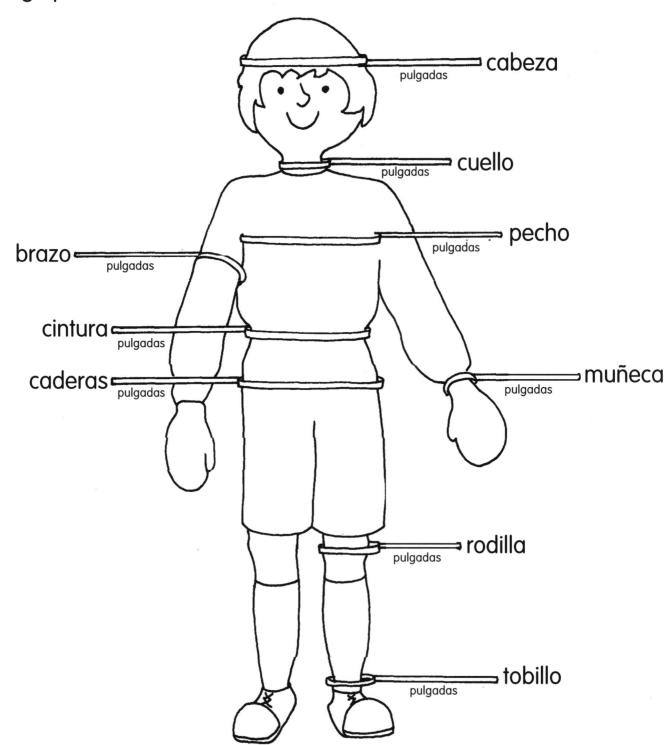

cabeza
pulgadas

cuello
pulgadas

pecho
pulgadas

brazo
pulgadas

cintura
pulgadas

caderas
pulgadas

muñeca
pulgadas

rodilla
pulgadas

tobillo
pulgadas

Beginning Reading Activities • EMC 5305

My Measurements

Use a tape measure and a friend
to find these measurements.

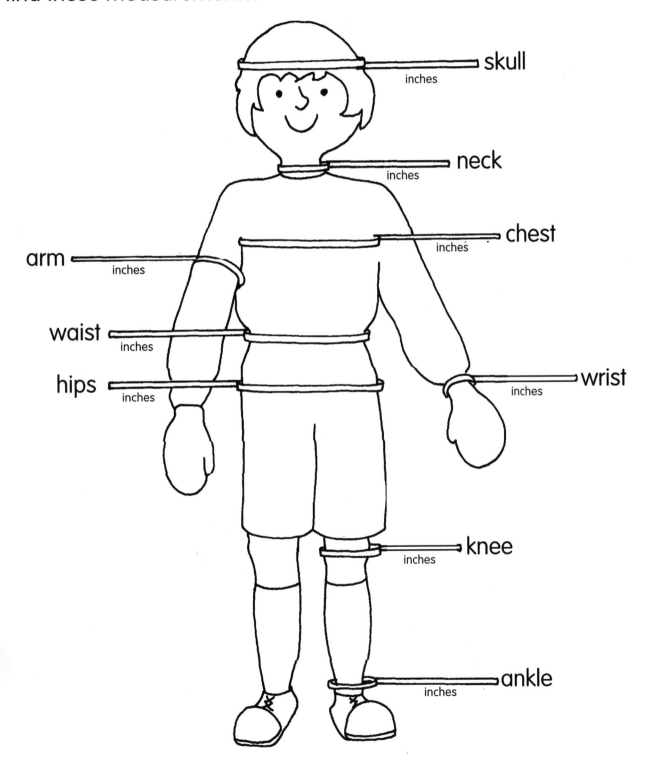

skull
inches

neck
inches

chest
inches

arm
inches

waist
inches

hips
inches

wrist
inches

knee
inches

ankle
inches

Nombre_____

Mi diario de crecimiento

Guarda este papel.
Usa una cinta para ver cuánto has crecido.
Escribe las pulgadas en la caja.
Escribe también la fecha.

pulgadas

pulgadas

pulgadas

pulgadas

pulgadas

Name_____

My Growth Diary

Save this paper.
Use a tape measure to see how tall you have grown.
Write the inches in the box.
Write the date, too.

inches

inches

inches

inches

inches

Date

¡Es estupendo ser único!

No hay ninguna otra persona en el mundo entero que sea exactamente como yo. Soy único. Eso quiere decir que no hay otra persona igual que yo. Me gusta como soy por muchas razones. Algunas de las razones son...

_____

_____

_____

_____

_____

_____

_____

Name_____

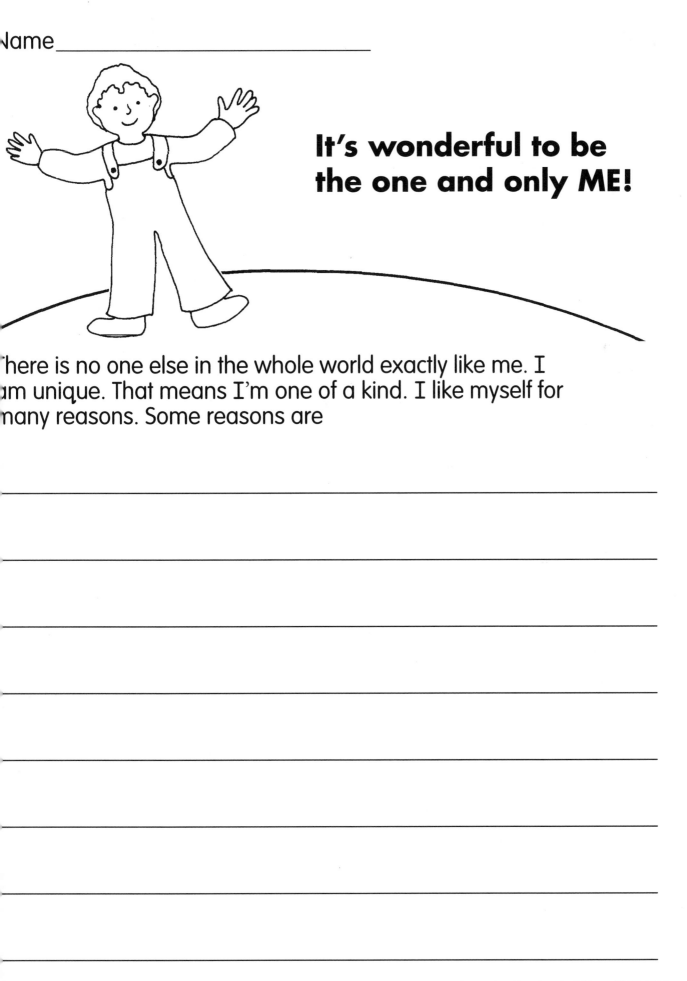

It's wonderful to be the one and only ME!

There is no one else in the whole world exactly like me. I am unique. That means I'm one of a kind. I like myself for many reasons. Some reasons are

_____

_____

_____

_____

_____

_____

_____

_____

Con la forma de mi barbilla,
y el color de mi mejilla,
¡no existe otro igual a mí!
De mi hombro a mi cintura,
con mi cara y mi figura,
¡no existe otro igual a mí!
Y aunque busque aquí y allá,
nadie como yo existirá
¡porque soy ÚNICO!
¡Es verdad!

J. E. Moore

Name_____

From my nose to my toes,
From my chin to my shin,
There is no one exactly like me.
From here at my waist
to my "sit-upon" place,
There is no one exactly like me.
Tho' you search far and near
I know you will find
There is no one like me.
I'm one of a kind!

J. E. Moore

 Beginning Reading Activities • EMC 5305

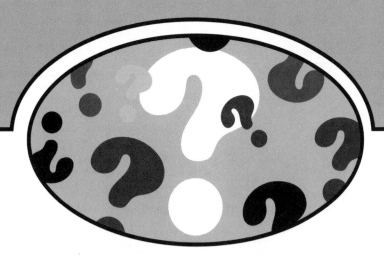

¿Quién? ¿Qué? ¿Dónde? ¿Cuándo?

Esta sección contiene 24 páginas en español con actividades para ayudar a los niños a aprender a identificar palabras que indican *quién, qué, cuándo* y *dónde*. Las actividades progresan en dificultad para apoyar a los niños en el desarrollo de destrezas como las siguientes:

- Reconocimiento de las partes de la oración por medio de terminología apropiada para su edad (*los nombres* son palabras que indican *quién* y *qué*; *los verbos* son *palabras que indican acción*; *las preposiciones* indican *dónde* y *cuándo*).
- Distinguir entre frases y oraciones completas.
- Uso correcto de mayúsculas y puntuación final al escribir oraciones.

Las actividades progresan en dificultad de la siguiente manera:

- Primero, los niños marcan palabras individuales o frases según lo que indican: *quién, cuándo, dónde* o si describen acción.
- Después, los niños marcan palabras en cada categoría dentro del contexto de oraciones completas.
- Luego, los niños leen una serie de frases para evaluar si responden a preguntas sobre *quién* o *qué*, *cuándo* o *dónde*, o si describen una acción.
- Finalmente, los niños organizan frases sueltas para formar oraciones lógicas, utilizando mayúsculas y puntuación correcta.

Who? What? Where? When?

This section contains 24 pages in English with activities to help students begin to identify words that tell *who, what, when,* and *where*. Activities are scaffolded to support students in developing the following skills:

- Ability to identify parts of speech through the use of age-appropriate terminology (*nouns* are words that tell *who* and *what***;** *verbs* are *action words*; *prepositions* are *when* and *where* words).
- Distinguishing between phrases and complete sentences.
- Correct use of initial capitals and end punctuation in writing sentences.

Activities progress in difficulty as follows:

- First, children mark individual words or phrases according to whether they tell *who, when,* or *where*, or if they describe action.
- Then, children mark words in each category within the context of complete sentences.
- Next, children read a series of phrases and evaluate whether they answer *who* or *what* questions, *when* or *where* questions, or describe an action.
- Finally, children organize discrete phrases into logical sentences, using correct capitalization and punctuation.

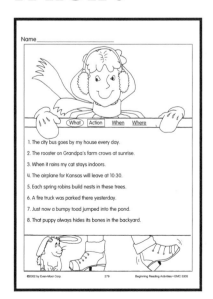

Nombre_____

Para personas, usamos la palabra QUIÉN.
Para cosas, usamos la palabra QUÉ.

Circula las palabras que indican QUIÉN. Subraya con una línea ondulada las palabras que indican QUÉ.

1. Paco

2. ese hombre

3. carreta roja chiquita

4. un elefante del circo

5. una bruja malvada

6. una tina sucia

7. Mujer Maravilla

8. millones de insectos

9. las puertas del castillo

10. zapatos viejos de tenis

11. tú y yo

12. un extranjero

13. helado de chocolate

14. cordones de zapato

15. su dentista

16. un dragón enojado

17. el payaso triste

18. mi mejor amigo

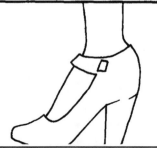
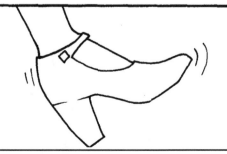

Name_____

People are WHO.

Things are WHAT.

Circle WHO words. Draw a wiggly line under WHAT words.

1. (Bill)

2. that man

3. little red wagon

4. circus elephant

5. a wicked witch

6. dirty bathtub

7. Wonder Woman

8. a million bedbugs

9. castle gates

10. old tennis shoes

11. you and me

12. a stranger

13. chocolate ice cream

14. broken shoelaces

15. his dentist

16. an angry dragon

17. the sad clown

18. my best friend

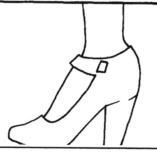
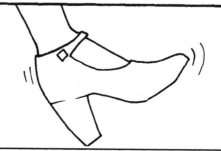

Beginning Reading Activities • EMC 5305

Bailar...
Patinar...
Nadar...

Haz un cuadrado alrededor de las palabras que indican ACCIÓN.

1. pasear
2. cantando
3. mesa
4. música
5. gateó
6. ayer
7. asomarse
8. chirriando
9. capturó

10. gritó
11. resbaló y se cayó
12. adentro
13. riéndose
14. zanahorias y chícharos
15. rebotó
16. deslizar
17. oso hormiguero
18. pintando

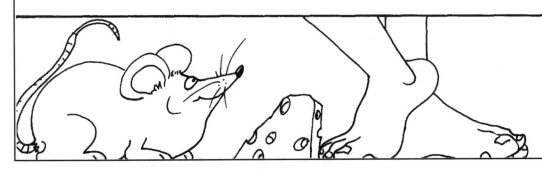

Dance...
Skate...
Swim...

Draw a box around the ACTION words.

1. ride
2. singing
3. table
4. music
5. crawled
6. yesterday
7. peeked
8. chirping
9. captured

10. screamed
11. slipped and fell
12. inside
13. giggling
14. carrots and peas
15. bounced
16. slither
17. anteater
18. painting

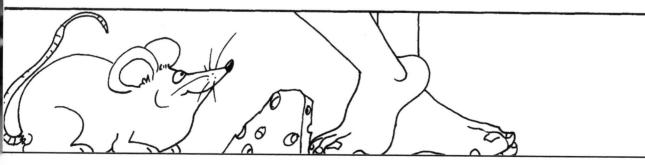

Beginning Reading Activities • EMC 5305

Nombre_____

Pon una línea debajo de las palabras que indican CUÁNDO.

1. <u>hace un minuto</u>

2. ayer

3. en el cuarto de Tomás

4. la semana pasada

5. allá

6. en la primavera

7. en sus vacaciones

8. 11:00

9. se alejó nadando

10. después de las clases

11. la semana que entra

12. en México

13. tenía un juguete

14. cuando crezca

15. el 25 de diciembre

16. en cualquier momento

17. adiós

18. érase una vez

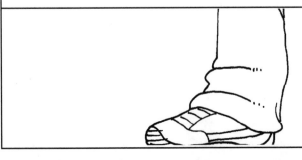
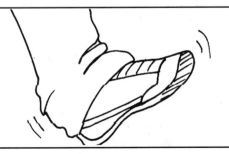

Draw one line under WHEN words.

1. <u>a minute ago</u>

2. yesterday

3. in Tom's room

4. last week

5. over there

6. in the spring

7. on her vacation

8. 11:00

9. swam away

10. after school

11. next week

12. in Mexico

13. had a toy

14. when I grow up

15. December 25

16. any minute now

17. good-bye

18. once upon a time

Pon dos líneas debajo de las palabras que indican DÓNDE.

1. <u>en la olla</u>

2. haz un pastel

3. encima del fregadero

4. en la casa del tío de José

5. en agosto

6. en la boca del hipopótamo

7. corre rápidamente

8. en el escritorio

9. entre Juan y Paco

10. cerca del parque

11. al lado del gallinero

12. en el segundo piso

13. a mi maestra

14. en un avión

15. entre tus oídos

16. en el día de mi cumpleaños

17. atrás del granero

18. en San Francisco

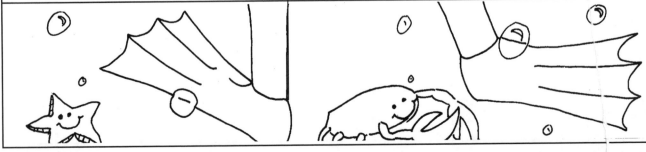

Draw two lines under WHERE words.

1. <u>in the pot</u>

2. make a cake

3. over the sink

4. at Uncle Joe's house

5. in August

6. in the hippo's mouth

7. run swiftly

8. on the desk

9. between Sam and Ned

10. near the park

11. by the henhouse

12. on the second floor

13. to my teacher

14. on an airplane

15. between your ears

16. on my birthday

17. behind the barn

18. in San Francisco

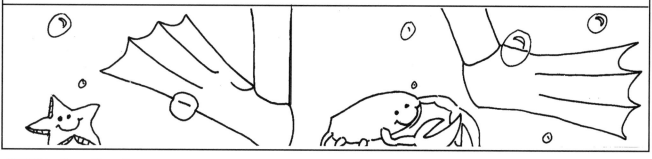

Nombre _____

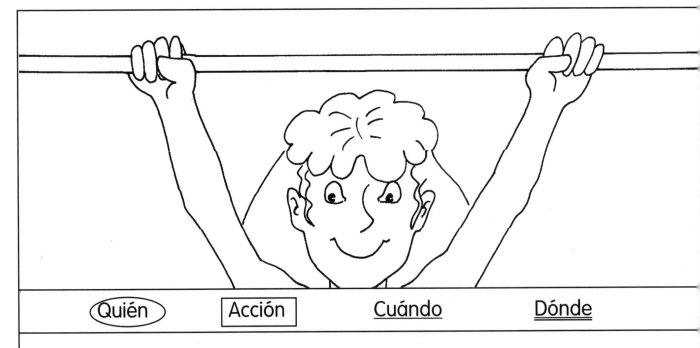

(Quién)   [Acción]   <u>Cuándo</u>   <u>Dónde</u>

1. la anciana

2. tosió

3. mañana

4. cerca del puente

5. el Príncipe Encantador

6. Mamá y Papá

7. gateó

8. pronto

9. en la fiesta

10. rascó

11. un carpintero cansado

12. un día de verano

13. anoche muy tarde

14. en el cielo

15. por la esquina

16. Sr. Jiménez

17. golpeó

18. se lanzó

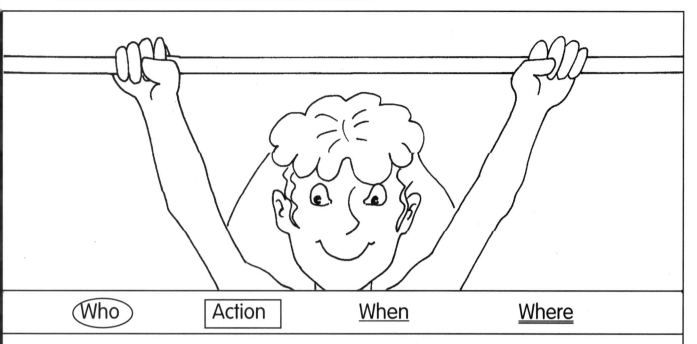

Who	Action	When	Where

1. the old lady

2. coughed

3. tomorrow

4. near the bridge

5. Prince Charming

6. Mom and Dad

7. crept

8. pretty soon

9. at the party

10. scratched

11. a tired carpenter

12. one summer day

13. late last night

14. in the sky

15. around the corner

16. Mr. Barnum

17. knocked

18. rushed

| Qué | Acción | Cuándo | Dónde |

1. en el piso de arriba

2. agarró

3. olió

4. en la cafetería

5. patineta

6. hace mucho

7. roncó

8. encima de su cabeza

9. camión de basura

10. después de las clases

11. detrás del librero

12. habló

13. cuando tenía seis años

14. pájaro cantor

15. en una tina

16. estaba cortando

17. algún día

18. perrito café chistoso

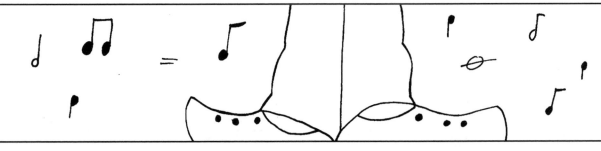

 Beginning Reading Activities • EMC 5305

Name_____

<u>What</u> | Action | <u>When</u>   <u>Where</u>

1. upstairs

2. caught

3. sniffed

4. in the cafeteria

5. skateboard

6. long ago

7. snored

8. over her head

9. garbage truck

10. after school

11. behind the bookshelf

12. spoke

13. when he was six

14. singing bird

15. in a bathtub

16. was cutting

17. someday

18. funny brown puppy

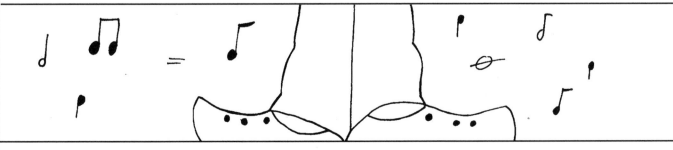

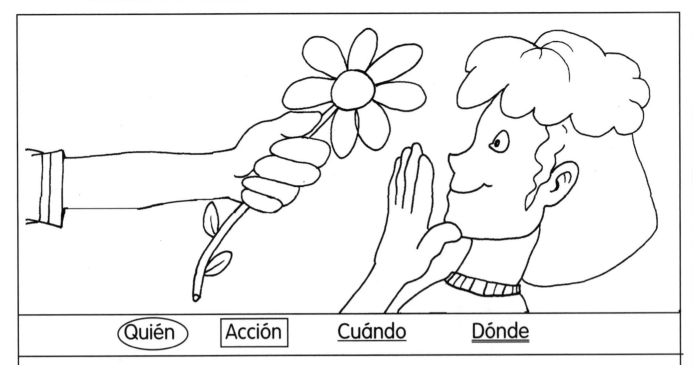

| Quién | Acción | Cuándo | Dónde |

1. El bebé de al lado lloró toda la noche.

2. El Halloween pasado, Jorge oyó ruidos extraños en el techo.

3. Ella comía apio con crema de cacahuate para el almuerzo todos los días.

4. Esta mañana, Felipe arregló su coche en nuestro garaje.

5. Mi abuela nació hace 60 años en Iowa.

6. Ayer una maestra joven celebró su cumpleaños.

7. Algún día, mi amigo y yo iremos a Disneylandia.

8. Los venados corren por este bosque todos los dias.

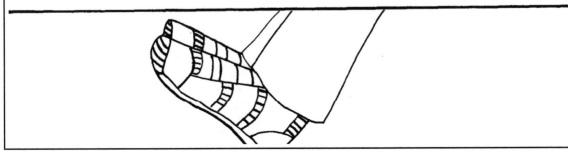

Name_____

(Who) [Action] <u>When</u> <u>Where</u>

1. The little baby next door cried all night.

2. Last Halloween, Jack heard strange noises on the roof.

3. She ate celery and peanut butter for lunch every day.

4. This morning Sam fixed his car in our garage.

5. My grandmother was born 60 years ago in Iowa.

6. A young teacher celebrated her birthday yesterday.

7. Someday my friend and I will go to Disneyland.

8. Deer run swiftly through these woods every day.

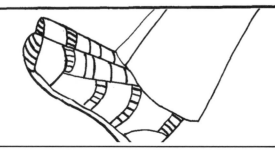

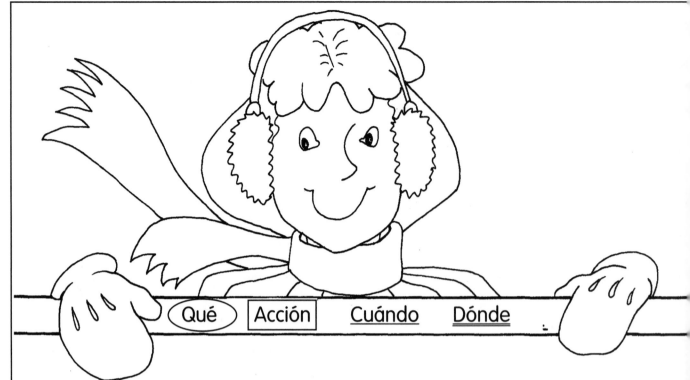

Qué   Acción   Cuándo   Dónde

1. El autobús de la ciudad pasa por mi casa todos los días.

2. El gallo en la granja de mi abuelo canta al salir el sol.

3. Cuando llueve, mi gato se queda adentro.

4. El avión a Kansas saldrá a las 10:30.

5. Cada primavera, los petirrojos construyen sus nidos en estos árboles.

6. Un camión de bomberos estaba estacionado allí ayer.

7. Hace un momento, un sapo saltó a la laguna.

8. Ese perrito siempre esconde sus huesos en el patio.

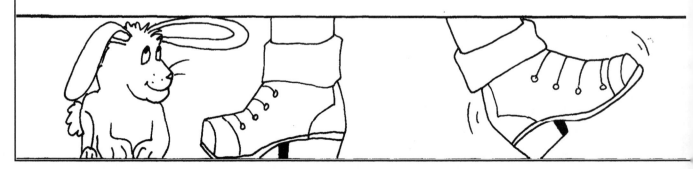

Name_____

(What) [Action] <u>When</u>   <u>Where</u>

1. The city bus goes by my house every day.

2. The rooster on Grandpa's farm crows at sunrise.

3. When it rains my cat stays indoors.

4. The airplane for Kansas will leave at 10:30.

5. Each spring robins build nests in these trees.

6. A fire truck was parked there yesterday.

7. Just now a bumpy toad jumped into the pond.

8. That puppy always hides its bones in the backyard.

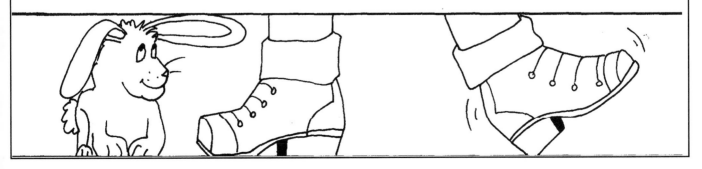

       Beginning Reading Activities • EMC 5305

Escribe la frase que contesta a la pregunta.

Cerca de las 12:00

comenzó a mordisquear una zanahoria

José

en el jardín del gigante.

¿Quién o qué? _____

¿Acción? _____

¿Cuándo? _____

¿Dónde? _____

Usa las frases (arriba) para hacer una oración completa.
Usa una letra mayúscula al principio y un punto al final.

_____

_____

_____

_____

Write each phrase after the question it answers.

About 12:00

began to nibble a carrot

Gus

in the giant's garden

Who or what? _____

Action? _____

When? _____

Where? _____

Make a sentence out of the parts.
Use a capital letter at the beginning and a period at the end.

_____

_____

_____

_____

Escribe la frase que contesta a la pregunta.

la lonchera de Carlos

se salió de

hace unos minutos

Una víbora

¿Quién o qué? _____

¿Acción? _____

¿Cuándo? _____

¿Dónde? _____

Usa las frases (arriba) para hacer una oración completa.
Usa una letra mayúscula al principio y un punto al final.

_____

_____

_____

_____

Write each phrase after the question it answers.

Bill's lunch box

slithered out of

a few minutes ago

A snake

Who or what? _____

Action? _____

When? _____

Where? _____

Make a sentence out of the parts.
Use a capital letter at the beginning and a period at the end.

_____

_____

_____

_____

Escribe la frase que contesta a la pregunta.

aterrizó en

un pájaro amarillo atrevido

Un día de primavera

la cabeza peluda de un oso

¿Quién o qué? _____

¿Acción? _____

¿Cuándo? _____

¿Dónde? _____

Usa las frases (arriba) para hacer una oración completa.
Usa una letra mayúscula al principio y un punto al final.

_____

_____

_____

_____

Write each phrase after the question it answers.

landed on

a bold yellow bird

One spring day

a bear's furry head

Who or what? _____

Action? _____

When? _____

Where? _____

Make a sentence out of the parts.
Use a capital letter at the beginning and a period at the end.

Escribe la frase que contesta a la pregunta.

Una noche oscura

causó un apagón

una tormenta

en la cueva de Horacio

¿Quién o qué? _____

¿Acción? _____

¿Cuándo? _____

¿Dónde? _____

Usa las frases (arriba) para hacer una oración completa.
Usa una letra mayúscula al principio y un punto al final.

_____

_____

_____

_____

Name_____

Write each phrase after the question it answers.

One dark night

caused the lights to go out

a storm

in Horace's cave

Who or what? _____

Action? _____

When? _____

Where? _____

Make a sentence out of the parts.
Use a capital letter at the beginning and a period at the end.

_____

_____

_____

_____

_____

Escribe la frase que contesta a la pregunta.

después de la puesta del sol

El extraterrestre

por la colina

se asomó

¿Quién o qué? _____

¿Acción? _____

¿Cuándo? _____

¿Dónde? _____

Usa las frases (arriba) para hacer una oración completa.
Usa una letra mayúscula al principio y un punto al final.

_____

_____

_____

_____

Write each phrase after the question it answers.

after the sun set

The space creature

the little hill

peeked over

Who or what? _____

Action? _____

When? _____

Where? _____

Make a sentence out of the parts.
Use a capital letter at the beginning and a period at the end.

_____

_____

_____

_____

_____

Escribe la frase que contesta a la pregunta.

miró en silencio

Dino

Cada noche

al cuarto de los niños

¿Quién o qué? _____

¿Acción? _____

¿Cuándo? _____

¿Dónde? _____

Usa las frases (arriba) para hacer una oración completa.
Usa una letra mayúscula al principio y un punto al final.

_____

_____

_____

_____

ame_____

Write each phrase after the question it answers.

stared quietly

Digby

Every night

into the children's room

Who or what? _____

Action? _____

When? _____

Where? _____

Make a sentence out of the parts.
Use a capital letter at the beginning and a period at the end.

_____

_____

_____

_____

Escribe la frase que contesta a la pregunta

bailó por

en la presentación de anoche

el escenario

La bailarina

¿Quién o qué? _____

¿Acción? _____

¿Cuándo? _____

¿Dónde? _____

Usa las frases (arriba) para hacer una oración completa.
Usa una letra mayúscula al principio y un punto al final.

_____

_____

_____

_____

Write each phrase after the question it answers.

danced around

at last night's show

the stage

The ballerina

Who or what? _____

Action? _____

When? _____

Where? _____

Make a sentence out of the parts.
Use a capital letter at the beginning and a period at the end.

_____

_____

_____

_____

Nombre_____

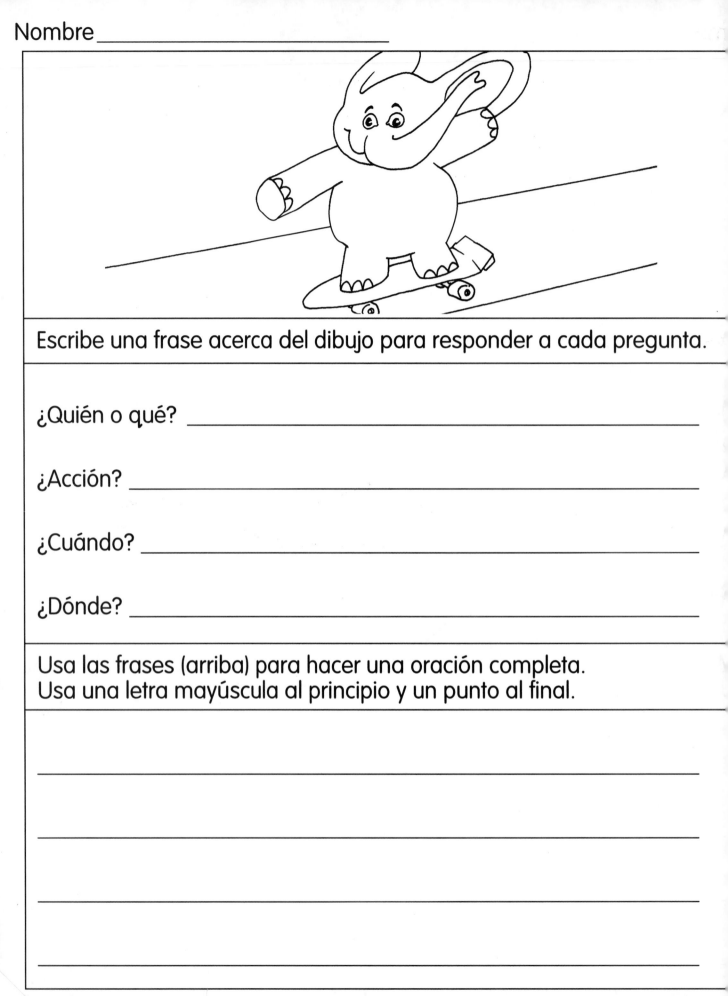

Escribe una frase acerca del dibujo para responder a cada pregunta.

¿Quién o qué? _____

¿Acción? _____

¿Cuándo? _____

¿Dónde? _____

Usa las frases (arriba) para hacer una oración completa.
Usa una letra mayúscula al principio y un punto al final.

_____

_____

_____

_____

ne_____

Write a phrase about the picture to answer each question.

Who or what? _____

Action? _____

When?_____

Where? _____

Make a sentence out of the parts.
Use a capital letter at the beginning and a period at the end.

_____

_____

_____

_____

Escribe una frase acerca del dibujo para responder a cada pregunta.

¿Quién o qué? _____

¿Acción? _____

¿Cuándo? _____

¿Dónde? _____

Usa las frases (arriba) para hacer una oración completa.
Usa una letra mayúscula al principio y un punto al final.

_____

_____

_____

_____

me_____

Write a phrase about the picture to answer each question.

Who or what? _____

Action? _____

When? _____

Where? _____

Make a sentence out of the parts.
Use a capital letter at the beginning and a period at the end.

_____

_____

_____

_____

_____

Nombre _____

Escribe una frase acerca del dibujo para responder a cada pregunta.

¿Quién o qué? _____

¿Acción? _____

¿Cuándo? _____

¿Dónde? _____

Usa las frases (arriba) para hacer una oración completa.
Usa una letra mayúscula al principio y un punto al final.

_____

_____

_____

_____

Write a phrase about the picture to answer each question.

Who or what? _____

Action? _____

When? _____

Where? _____

Make a sentence out of the parts.
Use a capital letter at the beginning and a period at the end.

_____

_____

_____

_____

Escribe una frase acerca del dibujo para responder a cada pregunta.

¿Quién o qué? _____

¿Acción? _____

¿Cuándo? _____

¿Dónde? _____

Usa las frases (arriba) para hacer una oración completa.
Usa una letra mayúscula al principio y un punto al final.

_____

_____

_____

_____

me_____

Write a phrase about the picture to answer each question.

Who or what? _____

Action? _____

When? _____

Where? _____

Make a sentence out of the parts.
Use a capital letter at the beginning and a period at the end.

_____

_____

_____

_____

Answer Key

Use the information on pages 302–304 to evaluate children's performance on the activities in this book.

Siguiendo Instrucciones/Following Instructions pages 3–65
Look at children's completed pages to evaluate whether they followed the instructions correctly.

Secuenciar instrucciones/Sequencing Directions pages 68–107
For each page, check to see that children have ordered the text as indicated:

page 68 Cómo comer una pizza
1. Corta la pizza en pedazos.
2. Levanta un pedazo.
3. Muerde la pizza.
4. ¡Lame tus labios!

page 69 How to Eat a Pizza
1. Cut the pizza into parts.
2. Pick up a slice.
3. Bite into the pizza.
4. Lick your lips!

page 70 Cómo usar el teléfono
1. Levanta el teléfono.
2. Marca el número que deseas.
3. Habla con tu amigo.
4. Cuelga el teléfono.

page 71 How to Use the Telephone
1. Pick up the telephone.
2. Call the number you want.
3. Talk to your friend.
4. Hang up the telephone.

page 72 Cómo dar de comer al gato
1. Toma una lata de comida para gatos y un plato.
2. Quita la tapa de la lata.
3. Pon la comida del gato en el plato.
4. Llama a tu gato.

page 73 How to Feed the Cat
1. Get a can of cat food and a dish.
2. Take the lid off the can.
3. Put the cat food in the dish.
4. Call your cat.

page 74 Cómo tomar leche
1. Toma un vaso. Luega, saca leche fría.
2. Llena todo el vaso.
3. Siéntate y bebe la leche.
4. Pon el vaso en el fregadero.

page 75 How to Drink Milk
1. Get a glass. Then get out the cold milk.
2. Fill the glass to the top.
3. Sit down and drink the milk.
4. Put the glass in the sink.

page 76 Cómo jugar con un yo-yo
1. Enrolla la cuerda del yo-yo.
2. Pon el extremo del hilo en tu dedo.
3. Deja caer al yo-yo y luego hazlo rebotar.
4. Repítelo muchas veces.

page 77 How to Work a Yo-Yo
1. Wind the string around the yo-yo.
2. Put the end of the string around your finger.
3. Drop the yo-yo, then pull it up.
4. Do this again and again.

page 78 Cómo hacer una máscara
1. Toma una bolsa grande de papel.
2. Ahora, dibuja una nariz y una boca.
3. Corta dos ojos para que puedas ver.
4. Ponte la máscara y sorprende a un amigo.

page 79 How to Make a Mask
1. Get a big brown bag.
2. Now draw a nose and a mouth.
3. Cut out two eyes so you can see.
4. Put on the mask and surprise your pal.

page 80 Cómo ponerse una chaqueta
1. Hace frío. Toma tu chaqueta.
2. Pon tus brazos en las mangas.
3. Sube el cierre de tu chaqueta.
4. Ahora puedes ir a jugar afuera.

page 81 How to Put on a Jacket
1. It is a cold day. Get your jacket.
2. Put your arms in the sleeves.
3. Zip up your jacket.
4. Now you can go out to play.

page 82 Cómo comer una galleta
1. Toma dos galletas de la caja.
2. Lleva tus galletas afuera y siéntate en la escalera del patio.
3. Cómelas a mordidas grandes.
4. Lámete los dedos.

page 83 How to Eat a Cookie
1. Take two cookies out of the box.
2. Take your cookies outside and sit on the back step.
3. Take big bites and eat them up.
4. Lick the last bits off your fingers.

page 84 Cómo montar a bicicleta
1. Súbete a la bicicleta.
2. Pon tus pies en los pedales y tus manos en el timón.
3. Empuja los pedales para avanzar por la calle.
4. Usa los frenos para parar.

page 85 How to Ride a Bike
1. Get on the bike.
2. Put your feet on the pedals and your hands on the handlebars.
3. Push the pedals so you can go down the street.
4. Put on the brakes to stop.

page 86 Cómo preparar un helado
1. Primero, busca una cuchara y un barquillo.
2. Después, saca el helado de la hielera.
3. Llena la cuchara con helado y ponlo en el barquillo.
4. Lame el helado y termínalo todo.

page 87 How to Make an Ice-Cream Cone
1. First get a scoop and a cone.
2. Then get the ice cream from the freezer.
3. Take a big scoop of ice cream and put it on the cone.
4. Take a big lick and gobble it down.

page 88 Cómo bañar a tu perro
1. Llena un balde con agua y toma una toalla grande.
2. Ahora, agarra a tu perro.
3. Pon a tu perro en el agua.
4. Lava con jabón a tu perro.
5. Enjuágalo.
6. Sécalo con una toalla grande y déjalo ir.

page 89 How to Give Your Dog a Bath
1. Fill a tub with water and get a big towel.
2. Now catch your dog.
3. Put him in the water.
4. Rub the suds all over your dog.
5. Wash the suds off the dog.
6. Dry him with the big towel and let him go.

page 90 Cómo pintar una cerca
1. Ponte ropa vieja.
2. Quita el polvo de la cerca.
3. Ahora toma una lata de pintura y un cepillo.
4. Pinta la cerca.
5. Revisa para ver si quedó alguna parte sin pintar.
6. Limpia el cepillo y guárdalo.

page 91 How to Paint a Fence
1. Dress in something old.
2. Wipe the dirt off the fence.
3. Now get a can of paint and a brush.
4. Brush the paint onto the fence.
5. Check for any spots you missed.
6. Clean the brush and put it away.

page 92 Cómo atrapar un renacuajo
1. Busca un frasco en tu casa.
2. Perfora la tapa del frasco.
3. Vete a una laguna.
4. Busca renacuajos en el agua.
5. Agarra algunos renacuajos en tu frasco.
6. Tapa el frasco y lleva los renacuajos a casa.

page 93 How to Catch a Tadpole
1. Find a jar at your house.
2. Put holes in the lid.
3. Go to a pond.
4. Look in the water until you see tadpoles.
5. Scoop up some tadpoles into your jar.
6. Put the lid on the jar and take them home.

page 94 Cómo recoger una manzana
1. Toma una bolsa y una escalera.
2. Pon la escalera cerca del árbol.
3. Sube la escalera.
4. Recoge las manzanas y ponlas en la bolsa.
5. Bájate de la escalera.
6. Lleva la bolsa de manzanas a la casa.

page 95 How to Pick an Apple
1. Get a bag and a ladder.
2. Put the ladder by the tree.
3. Go up the ladder.
4. Pick the apples and put them in the bag.
5. Go down the ladder.
6. Take the bag of apples into the house.

page 96 Cómo envolver un regalo
1. Pon el regalo en una caja.
2. Ahora tapa la caja.
3. Envuelve la caja con papel bonito.
4. Amarra la caja con cinta bonita.
5. Pon una tarjeta debajo de la cinta.
6. Lleva el regalo a la fiesta.

page 97 How to Wrap a Gift
1. Set the gift in a box.
2. Now put on the lid.
3. Wrap the box in pretty paper.
4. Tape a ribbon on the box.
5. Stick a card under the ribbon.
6. Take the gift to the party.

page 98 Cómo tender tu cama
1. Sal de la cama.
2. Arregla las sábanas.
3. Arregla la cobija.
4. Acomoda la almohada y ponla sobre la cama.
5. Pon el cubrecama encima.
6. Llama a tu mamá para que vea el trabajo que hiciste.

page 99 How to Make Your Bed
1. Get out of bed.
2. Pull up the sheets.
3. Fix the blanket.
4. Fluff the pillow and set it on the bed.
5. Put the bedspread on top.
6. Call your mom to see the good job you did.

page 100 Cómo hacer una linterna de calabaza
1. Escoge una calabaza anaranjada grande.
2. Córtale la parte de arriba.
3. Sácale todas las semillas.
4. Hazle ojos, nariz y boca.
5. Pon una vela en tu linterna.
6. Ponla en la ventana.

page 101 How to Make a Jack-o'-lantern
1. Pick a big orange pumpkin.
2. Cut off the top.
3. Take out all the seeds.
4. Cut out eyes, nose, and a mouth.
5. Put a candle in the jack-o'-lantern.
6. Set it in the window.

page 102 Cómo tomar un baño
1. Llena la tina con agua.
2. Echa espuma de baño al agua.
3. Métete a la tina.
4. Lávate con un paño y jabón.

5. Sal de la tina y sécate.
6. Vístete.

page 103 How to Take a Bath
1. Fill the tub with water.
2. Add bubble bath.
3. Get into the tub.
4. Wash with soap and a rag.
5. Get out of the tub and dry off.
6. Get dressed.

page 104 Cómo hacer un bocadillo
1. Saca el pan, la crema de cacahuate y un cuchillo.
2. Abre el frasco de crema de cacahuate.
3. Pon bastante crema de cacahuate en el pan.
4. Corta el bocadillo por la mitad.
5. Siéntate y dale una gran mordida.
6. ¡Cómetelo!

page 105 How to Make a Sandwich
1. Get out the bread, peanut butter, and a knife.
2. Open the jar of peanut butter.
3. Put lots of peanut butter on the bread.
4. Cut the sandwich in two.
5. Sit down and take a big bite.
6. Eat it up!

page 106 Cómo sembrar una semilla
1. Escoge las semillas que quieres sembrar.
2. Luego, abre un hoyo en la tierra.
3. Deja caer las semillas en el hoyo.
4. Cubre el hoyo con tierra.
5. Riega con agua las semillas.
6. Ahora las semillas podrán crecer.

page 107 How to Plant a Seed
1. Pick out the seeds you want to plant.
2. Next you must dig a hole in the dirt.
3. Drop the seeds into the hole.
4. Fill the hole with dirt and pat it down.
5. Water the seeds.
6. Now the seeds can grow.

Dibuja...luego, escribe/Draw...Then Write pages 110–170
Look at children's completed pictures and review their written responses to evaluate whether they completed these pages correctly.

Lee, piensa, corta y pega/Read, Think, Cut & Paste
pages 172–211
For each page, check to see that children have ordered the text as indicated below. Review written responses on reverse of each page to evaluate writing content and conventions (spelling, punctuation, capitalization, fluency).

page 172 Esta es una laguna grande.
Hay un tronco en la laguna.
Una rana verde está sobre el tronco.
Salta al agua, rana.

page 173 This is a big pond.
A log is in the pond.
A green frog is on the log.
Jump into the water, frog.

page 174 "Ven aquí, Puerquito. Es la hora de tu baño."
"Te va a gustar. No intentes escapar."
"¿No es divertido el baño, Puerquito? ¡Qué bien te verás!"
"¡Cuidado! Mira cómo has regado el agua."

page 175 "Come here, Chipper. It is time for your bath."
"You will like it. Do not try to get away."
"Isn't this fun, Chipper? How nice you will look."
"Look out! What a mess you have made."

page 176 Susi huele algo rico.
Susi comienza a escarba. La tierra vuela a todas partes.
¡Qué hueso tan grande encontró. ¡Qué rico! ¡Qué rico!
Susi comió un buen almuerzo. Ahora va a descansar.

page 177 Sniff, sniff, sniff. Sid smelled something good.
Sid began to dig. Dirt went all over.
What a big bone he found. Yum, yum, yum.
Sid had a good lunch. Now he will rest.

page 178 Vivo cerca de una laguna.

Nado todo el día.
Juego con mis amigos.
Me meto debajo del agua para comer.

page 179
I live by a pond.
I swim around all day.
I play with my friends.
I duck under the water to eat.

page 180
Coco es una perra feliz.
Tiene un patio grande donde puede jugar.
Ve un pájaro pasar volando.
Se sienta en un lugar soleado y menea su cola.
Persigue a una mariposa por todo el patio.

page 181
Coco is a happy dog. She has a big yard to play in.
She sees a bird go by.
She sits in a sunny spot and wags her tail.
She runs across the yard after a butterfly.

page 182
"Quiero un trabajo. Preguntaré aquí," dijo Kiwi.
"Quiero trabajar." "¿Cómo me puede ayudar un kiwi?"
preguntó el Sr. Lara.
"Puedo ayudar de esta manera," dijo Kiwi.
Kiwi no consiguió el trabajo. Se fue triste.

page 183
"I want a job. I will ask in here," said Kiwi.
"I want a job." "How can a kiwi help me?" asked Mr. Green.
"I can help this way," said Kiwi.
Kiwi did not get the job. He went away sad.

page 184
"Hola, Sr. Oso." "No soy un oso."
"¿Qué está comiendo, Sr. Oso?" "¡Yo NO soy un oso!"
"¿Por qué se va, Sr. Oso?" "¡No soy un OSO! ¡Soy un panda!"
"¡Oh! No lo sabía y ya se fue el Sr. Panda."

page 185
"Hello, Mr. Bear." "I am not a bear."
"What are you eating, Mr. Bear?" "I am NOT a bear!"
"Why are you running away, Mr. Bear?" "I'm not a BEAR!
I'm a panda!"
"Oh! I did not know, and now Mr. Panda has gone away."

page 186
"Quiero salir, pero debo hacer mis quehaceres primero."
Doña Pata arregló su cama rápidamente.
También lavó los trastes.
"Ahora puedo salir de compras," dijo Doña Pata.

page 187
"I want to go out, but I must do my chores first."
Mrs. Wig-Wag quickly made her bed.
She did the dishes, too.
"Now I can go out and shop," said Mrs. Wig-Wag.

page 188
A Nena le gusta nadar en el agua.
Puede zambullirse para agarrar una almeja.
Nena golpea la almeja con una piedra para romper la concha.
Ahora puede comer la almeja.

page 189
Otto likes to swim in the water.
He can dive down to get a clam.
Otto hits the clam with a rock to crack the shell.
Now he can eat the clam.

page 190
Chiquita iba a visitar a una amiga.
Llegó a un charco demasiado grande para cruzar.
Chiquita miraba a todos lados. "Ya sé qué hacer," dijo ella.
"Haré un barquito." Y así lo hizo.

page 191
Little Huggy Bug was on her way to visit a friend.
She came to a puddle that was too big to cross.
Little Huggy Bug looked around. "I know what to do," she said.
"I will go on a boat." And she did.

page 192
Camilo se sentía mal. Le dolía un diente.
"Vamos al dentista. Él lo arreglará," dijo Mamá.
El dentista arregló el diente.
Ahora Camilo puede cortar árboles de nuevo.

page 193
Bud felt bad. His tooth hurt.
"We will go to the dentist. He will fix it," said Mom.
The dentist did fix the tooth.
Now Bud can cut down trees again.

page 194
"¿Quién eres? ¿Eres nuevo aquí en el árbol?"
"¡Despierta! ¡Despierta! ¡Ya oscureció! ¡Levántate!"
"Ay, ¿qué he hecho? ¿Sabrá volar?"
"¡Buen viaje! Vuelve a visitarme algún día."

page 195
"Who are you? Are you new to this tree?"
"Wake up, wake up! It's dark. Time to get up!"
"Oh, what have I done? Can it fly?"
"Have a good trip. Come and see me again."

page 196
"Los huevos están pintados y aún me sobra pintura."
"Ya sé qué haré. Pintaré las flores."
"¿Puedes ayudarme, Pájaro? Esto es divertido."
"Qué bonitas se ven las flores ahora."

page 197
"The eggs are painted and I have this paint left."
"I know what I will do. I will paint the flowers."
"Can you help me, Bird? It is fun."
"How pretty the flowers look now."

page 198
¡Pum, pum! "Este es un trabajo difícil."
"¡Ay, ay! ¡No salpiques la pintura!"
"Ahora podemos guardar las herramientas."
"Qué casa nueva tan bonita!"

page 199
Bang, bang, bang. "This is hard work."
"Oh, oh. Do not splash the paint."
"We can put the tools away now."
"What a pretty new house."

page 200
"Por favor, dos boletos para la función de magia."
"¿Nos sentamos aquí? Quiero ver todos los trucos."
"Les presentaré un truco de magia."
"¡Mira! ¡Qué truco tan gracioso!"

page 201
"Two tickets for the magic show, please."
"Can we sit here? I want to see all of the magic show."
"I will do a magic trick for you."
"Oh, look! What a funny trick."

page 202
"Mira! Gitano salió de su jaula."
"Allí está Gitano, sobre la pipa de Papá. ¡Vamos a agarrar
"Ven, Gitano. Hay algo rico aquí."
"Gitano está feliz en su jaula. Oye cómo canta."

page 203
"Look! Flash is out of his cage."
"There is Flash on Dad's pipe. Let's catch him!"
"Come here, Flash. Here is something good."
"Flash is happy to be back. He is singing."

page 204
"Mira las lindas conchas. Quisiera tenerlas en mi casa."
"Esto tardará bastante tiempo."
"Yo puedo ayudarte, amiguito. Tengo muchos brazos."
"Gracias. Eres un buen amigo."

page 205
"Look at these pretty shells. I wish I had them at my
house."
"This will take a long time."
"I can help you, little friend. I have many arms."
"Thank you. You are a good friend."

page 206
"¿Qué puedo hacer en este día de sol?" preguntó
la hormiga Ana.
"Invita a tus amiguitos a ir de excursión," dijo la Sra.
Hormiga.
Ana invita a todos sus amiguitos para ir a almorzar al par
"Es divertido ir de excursión al parque con los amigos,"
dijo Ana.

page 207
"What can I do this sunny day?" asked Ann Ant.
"Ask your friends to go on a picnic," said Mrs. Ant.
So Ann invited all of her friends to a picnic in the park.
"It's fun to picnic in the park with friends," laughed Ann.

page 208
El piloto caminó hacia su avión.
Se subió al asiento del piloto.
El avión avanzó por la pista.
Es divertido volar por las nubes.

page 209
The pilot went to his airplane.
He jumped into the cockpit.
The airplane went down the runway.
It is fun to fly in and out of the clouds.

page 210
Algo le molestaba a la culebra Samuel. Le picaba la piel.
Samuel reptaba por las piedras y debajo de los troncos.
Toda la piel vieja se cayó.
Por fin, Samuel se sintió mejor. Se fue a buscar algo
de comer.